THE FAMILY
IN DIALOGUE

THE FAMILY
IN DIALOGUE

REVISED EDITION

A. DONALD BELL

ZONDERVAN PUBLISHING HOUSE
GRAND RAPIDS, MICHIGAN

To

Judy

Who made our family complete

CONTENTS

PREFACE

1. COURTSHIP AND ENGAGEMENT.................... 13
   ". . . dialogue begins"

2. THE HONEYMOON AND FIRST MONTHS 31
   ". . . duologue of love"

3. THE PARENT OF THE CHILD 43
   ". . . non-verbal response, questions and answers,
   and discourse"

4. THE PARENT OF THE TEEN-AGER 64
   ". . . communication — not investigation"

5. THE FAMILY TOGETHER......................... 84
   ". . . open forum"

6. THE PRODUCTIVE YEARS.........................113
   ". . . conversation vs. preoccupation"

7. THE LATER YEARS...............................133
   ". . . monologue — the silent spot"

8. DIVORCE 147

APPENDIX. The Church and Family Life Education.....159
   Family Counseling and Resources
   Church Programs in Family Guidance

BIBLIOGRAPHY 169

INDEX 179

Preface

"WHAT CAUSED OUR MARRIAGE TO FAIL? Why were not our children self-reliant? Where did we miss our opportunities to give them a real spiritual foundation? How is it that, later, they didn't take marriage seriously? What about the two of us in retirement?"

These questions are too frequently asked in our time. Are there some practical, helpful answers? Yes. Most of the helps are like beads, however, because they are all threaded on one underlying solution — communication!

LACK OF COMMUNICATION

After twenty-one years of experience in the field of marriage and family counseling, I still find communication the basic problem in this area.

Some say unfaithfulness is the basic reason for the breakdown in marriage. But it is not just the unfaithfulness; it is the lack of communication in trying to work out situations which actually bring about the break. On the other hand, others say that lack of spirituality in the home is a cause of breakdown, and yet communication and its exercise is the secret of spiritual health within the family.

One of the great psychiatrists of our day, Dr. Viktor Frankl, says our basic sin today is what he calls "God-shyness." By this he means that we are afraid to talk about spiritual things even within the intimacies of our family circle. So here we get back to the basic problem of communication.

We call this problem basic, because it is fundamental to all the other areas. To clarify this point, listed on the next page is a layman's list of practical rules for success in marriage and family life. As you read through them, notice how many relate to this issue of communication.

(1) Maintain an equality of respect for one another.

(2) Eliminate needless irritability and sources of antagonism.

(3) Do not cherish feelings of resentment.

(4) Keep looking for new ways to do and say things.

(5) Remember the little courtesies of life.

(6) Be partners in every area of life and talk about it often.

(7) Do not both get angry at the same time.

(8) Make the best of whatever life brings.

(9) Plan finances together.

Poor Preparation for Marriage

Someone has said that the secret of a good marriage, as with most everything else in life, is solid and well-grounded preparation. We are tempted to be idealistic and teach that a Christian home is easy to establish. We take successful families for granted — we forget that tidal waves of opposition assail a Christian home.

Establishing a Christian home is impossible when only human resources are employed; this great enterprise calls for God as a partner. Founding, growing, and structuring a Christian home is nothing short of a miracle in this world! We expect more out of marriage than any group of people in the history of the race — we expect a miracle!

Yet, here again, our youngsters are ignorant about these facts because the facts have not been discussed with them. The family and church must talk about the wholesome positive aspects of love and marriage.

Lack of Stimulating Goals

Like any other partnership or "team" activity, there must be a constant goal toward which the individual team members work.

The coach is constantly setting up intermediate goals —
"We must win the next conference game." Then he sets up
ultimate goals "We must win the conference title." So it is
in marriage and family life. Saving money to buy something
which the whole family will enjoy is psychologically more
sound than paying it off on the installment plan.

Also, the family planning of the annual vacation can become an immediate goal which is stimulating to good family
life. The family's concern about winning one member to
Christ can also become a goal for the family.

Needless to say, many of these goals must be spiritual in
nature. And it is the responsibility of the parents to keep
them before the family group.

No Spiritual Focal Point

As we have just indicated, a healthy family needs goals
to keep interest, stimulation, and devotion in the family
circle. All of this finds its consummation in one final spiritual focal point. This is constantly defined and refined before the family in personal devotion, in family "discussion."

As a unit, the family should be living toward the goal of
becoming the maximum Christian home. Many homes break
down because the only ultimate goals are material and financial.

Thus the ingredients of a happy, successful family are like
those in a good cake. They must be the right elements, mixed
correctly, and pressed into the mixture in the correct sequence and in the right fashion. Many of the ingredients of
a happy home are put into the very foundation. Then at
various intervals others are added to the main body, and
thus the superstructure which we call the Christian home
is built.

These ingredients are potent in happy family life when
they are communicated. Meaningful dialogue can help bring
solutions in the problem areas of poor preparation for mar-

riage, lack of goals, and missing spiritual emphases. The following chapters seek to assist in these trouble zones.

It is hoped that this volume will be beneficial to parents, pastors, workers in religious education, and young people themselves. Family experiences are presented in a rather developmental order: friendship, courtship, romance, engagement, marriage, the child, the teenager, the family as a group, and the adult as he matures. Some discussion is devoted to the single adult and to the retired person. Emphasis is placed on the need for dialogue between family members as well as conversation between home and church. The final section of the book provides aids for family counseling and suggestions for family life emphases in churches.

The writer is grateful to his parental and present family as well as to the many wonderful Christian homes in the churches and schools where he has served.

A. DONALD BELL

1. Courtship and Engagement

". . . dialogue begins"

IT COULD HAVE HAPPENED. . . . Judy Beal, a typical thirteen-year-old, might be given in marriage by her parents to a forty-year-old man she has never seen.

Grace Smith, an average teenager, could be waiting impatiently for her parents, the marriage broker, and the parents of some unknown man to decide about her marriage.

Evelyn McQuade conceivably could be sold as a bride to a tyrant who would be called her "husband." The marriage could be for business or political advantages.

These three girls could be in these situations today were it not for our Judeo-Christian heritage as it has resulted in the American pattern of preparation for marriage! It could have happened.

Deep feelings of love have not always been as freely expressed as they are among young people today. The language of expression has not always been known either.

Young people in our country should stand in awe at the privileges they enjoy. Meeting many young people (eligible

13

and ineligible); courting; falling in love; and freely decid-
ing about marriage are unique, sacred privileges of our culture. One can see that it would be impossible to account for
the significant place of dialogue in these emerging courtship
privileges. The whole process of meeting other young people
and gradually narrowing these contacts down to one person
is based on the personality exchange which grows out of
conversation.

Reuel L. Howe says, "Love is born out of (this) love in
which there is both the intimacy of what these two people
share in common and the distance of the unplumbed mystery of each. The emergence of this mutual awareness in the
relationship reveals an important distinction between mono-
logical and dialogical love."[1] Personality adjustments and
wholesome social contacts comprise the "genesis" of this cultural plan.

Our Process of Friendship, Dating, Courtship, and Engagement

It is a pyramidal development and usually follows a rather
fixed pattern and sequence, something like this:

1) The American child is placed in a heterogeneous, yet
graded, group in school, church, or neighborhood. His first
conversational and social contacts are usually with his own
sex. For example, the church party for primaries begins
with the boys gathering on one side of the room. They appear to ignore the girls. As a defense mechanism the girls
begin to converse and giggle among themselves. Soon the
interaction between the boys becomes dull since attention
spans are still short. Then, one little boy attempts to stand
on his head in order to get the attention of the girls. The
girls, in turn, giggle loud so as to attract the boys.

2) Still later in life boys and girls begin to attract one

---

[1] Howe, Reuel L., *The Miracle of Dialogue* (New York: The Seabury Press, 1964), p. 7.

another. It is at this time that little Kenny gets a coke for little Karla at the birthday party. Such an act can open the way for simple verbalization with little real conversation. Teasing by peers will periodically retard this development, but it still progresses.

3) For a long period these few contacts between young boys and girls are not very selective. This is good, since each youngster begins to learn to carry on simple conversation with many types of growing personalities. The quiet boy begins dialogical adjustment with a talkative little girl. She learns how to draw him out. The vast diversity of activities in which these children engage enhances these opportunities. Thus, the social need for conversation helps to bring about personality adjustment and improvement. Observation of the marked differences in people is revealing to these children. This is evidenced by their attempts to "type" or "pigeon-hole" each other.

4) Before long a degree of selection develops. Out of this free and permissive atmosphere a boy becomes more interested in a certain girl. He selects her for his partner in party games and repeatedly gets her refreshments. Communication between these two becomes more fluid and versatile. They now converse freely and can make meaningful contact through facial and eye expression — those arts so needed in marriage some day. Also, boys and girls now develop more common interests — this provides subject matter for dialogue.

5) Although interest still shifts from one child to another, the beginnings of "dating" finally come in our system. Perhaps, Johnny is going to a Sunday school party and his father is to drive him. He may ask his father to take a little girl friend along and other "couples" are also included. Even though the two may not remain together all evening, the characteristics of the American date are in evidence. As developmental levels emerge, the accompanying skills enable these children to reach new heights of conversation and so-

phistication (cf. R. J. Havighurst's theory of developmental tasks).

6) Now a period of "group" and "double dating" begins. This level of social contact is still closely chaperoned and informal. In the meantime, however, the youngsters have learned some of the social graces and habits. These points of courting etiquette become vehicles for easier conversation. Complex dialogue about school games, church activities, and neighborhood gossip forms. Conversation becomes more structured due to stabilization of personality. As each personality grows, viewpoints and opinions make conversation and contact more lively. The adjustments here are excellent preparation for marriage.

7) Adolescent development, in our society, brings the privilege and responsibility of dating (in the group at first) without a chaperone. This brings ever-changing situations which stimulate conversation and adjustment. Psycho-social, as well as physical, "distance" between couples must be handled. At first, young people should continue to "play the field" in dating. This continues the training program for marriage preparation.

8) At last, the right time for individual dating comes. New adjustments are demanded socially. Conversation may be more difficult too. Tests have proven, however, that young people who have had more contacts with other youngsters handle this situation better. Yet, there is no experience comparable to the first confrontation of a boy and girl alone. The struggles for meaningful dialogue, and the attempts at real understanding are difficult.

If the adolescent has been well guided previously, these first single dates will be with youngsters who are compatible and who "speak the same language." If a teenager has made contacts in a wholesome church group he will date one of his peers. Parents and leaders have, therefore, some control.

9) After years of single and group dating our cultural

procedure in courtship has the young person ready for selectivity. He knows how to communicate and adjust to different kinds of persons. His own personhood has developed on the basis of this background; what he feels to be God's will in selection; his understanding of and involvement in love; and his search for his life partner. He usually makes a mutual agreement with this girl which we call "going steady." To have done so with another girl before this time might have retarded the developmental plan. Good personality and communicative growth does not take place in this type of dating. "Going steady" should probably be reserved as the step before engagement. This is true from both psychological and social standpoints.

10) The final stage in our American plan is what we call engagement. Commonplace though it may seem to us, engagement is rather unique in world history. This period of commitment is the time for closer adjustment, deep and very specific dialogue, and spiritual involvement. The varnish of "talk" must be removed and two people may now freely and honestly "commune." All of the communicative skills which the two people have learned are, at this point, put to test. "Every man is a potential adversary, even those whom we love. Only through dialogue are we saved from this enmity toward one another. Dialogue is to love what blood is to the body."[2]

The subject matter of this conversation is new also. Deep feelings and convictions about marriage itself, spiritual beliefs and implications, children, material needs and desires, social attitudes, personal and intimate frustrations, family problems, and ultimate life goals are discussed. Local peer gossip, fads, school and neighborhood news, and "small talk" become secondary. Dr. W. Perry Crouch, experienced pastor-counselor, writes, "Several worthy statements could be listed under the purpose of a formal engagement period. It is a

[2] *Ibid.*

time for a final examination of your love. It is a time when
other suitors are eliminated. It is the announcement of an
intent to marry. It anticipates a life together. It is a time
for the careful consideration of the definite factors involved
in marriage, such as finances, living quarters, children, church
relationship, and family ties. It is a time to make a final
checkup about ideals, family background, personality traits,
emotional maturity, and similar things."[3] Thus, specific plans
for marriage and family living are honestly detailed.

This rather informal sequence constitutes our system of
preparation for marriage. In short it develops personality as
well as marriage readiness.

ADOLESCENT PERSONALITY DEVELOPMENT

A discussion of adolescent personality development is now
necessary for us to grasp the real significance of the preparation for marriage.

Personality is the showcase of what is going on in the
young person's mind. He must be aware of this without
becoming self-conscious about his personality development.
This self-consciousness probably will not take place if he has
a clear understanding of what personality is. Many of our
young people think of personality almost as something they
wear or put on their backs. They think of personality as being almost consistent with physical appearance. The wise
parent will help them to see that personality begins at the
heart and that physical appearance is only the outward expression of it. This teaching is not always easy to implement
since the young person's contacts with his peers have emphasized the physical development.

Several things will be of help in guiding into an understanding of what personality is. (1) Personality is the greatest power in the world. The maturing young person needs

[3] W. Perry Crouch, *Guidance for Christian Home Life* (Nashville, Tennessee: Convention Press, 1955), p. 101.

to understand the stewardship of life involved in his personality development. (2) There are no perfect personalities. There will be flaws in all of us, but those things which motivate our lives can have more influence upon our personalities than anything else. Therefore, when the young woman thinks clean thoughts and has high ideals, she will naturally radiate a lovable and attractive personality. A young man who desires honesty and trustworthiness becomes this kind of person.

(3) Personality develops rapidly in group experiences. Parents should provide ample and various opportunities for group activity among the young men and women. No single area of life, with the exception of spiritual ideals, has more to do with personality development than the social. Family contacts and interpersonal relations are also significant, of course.

(4) "Maturity" means that the young person will gradually come to the place where he gets more satisfaction out of doing for others and giving to others than he does out of receiving. It means that the parent has the blessed privilege of taking a human personality at the time when it is wrapped up in itself and leading it to a fuller development — a healthy concern for the welfare of others. This type of development is the perfect preparation for marriage or a career. In addition, the family, church, school, and community offer formal helps for young people. This will be discussed later.

Some education, unfortunately, is not so constructive. Someone has said that most of the preparation for marriage young Americans receive is that which they get in sarcastic jokes and smutty stories. Such a declaration is at least partly true. What can be done to remedy this situation?

GUIDANCE THROUGH THE PROCESS

For generations the home has been the chief center of responsibility for counseling young people in the preparation for Christian marriage. (For a discussion of the layman in marriage counseling see John W. Drakeford, *Counseling for Church Leaders,* Nashville, Tennessee: Broadman Press, 1961, p. 116.) Some homes have done an excellent job; others have failed miserably. Then the public schools entered the program and began to provide some fine assistance (in terms of course work and co-curricular activities) in the preparation for wholesome married life.

In recent years the government has made available excellent literature and some programming. In fact, many vocational counselors who work in preparation for marriage receive government help for these services through our public schools. National emphases also have helped to solve the problem. National Family Week has made its contribution, and various wholesome agencies and organizations have tried to contribute from various viewpoints.

However, we are now faced squarely with the fact that the churches must take their stand and project this program also. Some churches are already at work, and various means have been employed. For example, many churches have incorporated in their annual Christian home emphasis conferences for engaged young people. Here, under the direction of a capable leader, discussions are held; and if these groups are small, frank and intimate growth can take place.

Also, a number of churches have made the most of the excellent material in current Sunday school lessons and other programs on marriage. After class or program discussion in young people's groups, extended sessions have been planned. For example, one church, when material for preparation for marriage was in the Sunday school lesson, scheduled some subsequent meetings for its young people after church on Sunday evenings. These discussions continued for some time and proved to be highly beneficial.

In the college church additional opportunities of this type are often provided. Frequently youth workers in the local church and the college arrange fellowship and discussion periods for single young people. Workers in these two areas today are usually experienced, trained, and qualified in preparation for marriage. Also, college students are frequently in environments where they are thinking about marriage, and this makes a good atmosphere for such training. Another advantage in these areas is, of course, the availability of college personnel who teach and work in the counseling field.

Some of our large churches offer classes in preparation for marriage, with the pastor meeting regularly with couples who are engaged. Naturally, this does not substitute for his personal counseling with the couple immediately before their marriage time.

One of the new tasks of counseling in preparation for marriage is that of the church staff youth worker. Many times he deals with young people as they have met each other and fallen in love. He merits their respect and he is logically the one they will first approach. Then, of course, he will want to refer them to their pastor.

The last suggestion in this area concerns pre-marriage guidance by the pastor. This has come to be traditional in modern church life and is one of the best avenues of aid available. Some pastors counsel in a rather informal way; others have developed a fuller program and begin to deal with the couple when they are first engaged. (See Wayne E. Oates, *Premarital Pastoral Care and Counseling*, Nashville, Tennessee: Broadman Press, 1955.)

Some pastors have even gone so far as to give simple tests that indicate readiness for marriage. This can be done satisfactorily, if the pastor is trained and skilled in this area. Other pastors work in conjunction with fellow counselors in the church community on a consulting basis.

We all need to work together — wisely and tactfully — to provide for our young people wise and sifted information as they prepare to establish Christian homes. The church and its auxiliaries, and other agencies have increasingly enriched their programs in this area. We are fast coming to the day where the typical, active church will be providing considerable assistance to its young people as they approach married life.

THE LANGUAGE OF LOVE

The social, psychological, spiritual guidance of young people must involve an understanding of love. If love is missing, human relationships of all kinds are like bodies without blood. During courtship and engagement love is the great essential. Preparation for marriage requires a growing awareness of the characteristics of true love. Persons contemplating marriage must have some understanding of how love is "fed and matured."

Love is the most important relationship in all of life; yet, too few of us understand it. Webster's Collegiate Dictionary says that love is "a feeling of strong personal attachment induced by sympathetic understanding or by ties of kindred; ardent affection. The benevolence attributed to God as being like a father's affection for his children; men's adoration of God. Strong liking; fondness; good will; as, love of learning; love of country." Although some of these definitions and others indicate an outside motivation toward love (like kinship or relationship), true love is spontaneous. Therefore, the personal evaluation of our loves — for fiance, for God, for our brothers, and for family members ought to be experienced.

An inventory of our loves might involve answers to the following questions:

Do I return love? Love may begin as a one-way street; but true love looks forward to fulfillment in a two-way exchange. Romantic love must always be returned. The Bible says that God first loved us. Yet, the process is not complete until we return that love. Therefore, spiritual love is the same. I first love an unsaved person enough to tell him about Christ, but after he becomes a Christian he returns my friendship and Christian love. A one way friendship ought not to go on forever. A Christian must both love and be lovable. His colleagues accept him when their relationship is based on a two-way path of sincere, brotherly love. This "commerce" of Christian love becomes the spiritual "lubrication" between the mechanical parts of the machine of human relations.

The engagement period is a time for this exchange of love on a high and sincere level. This matures the two people and cements the relationship.

Do I try to force love? Love cannot be coerced. A "forced" love is a dead love. I can't demand that people love me. Marriages fail when attempts are made to force love. Even God gives us the power to refuse His love. One must build love by feeding it. We can urge, exhort, encourage, and persuade — but not demand. "Being lovable" is the only real answer.

Do I express love regularly? Love, since it is a living and growing thing, must be expressed (fed) regularly. Here, again, we find the significance of conversation—"the dialogue of love." Also, if my loving attitude is consistently expressed in deeds, I increase romantic love. Even as our personal love to Christ must be shown in consistent service, church attendance, and daily prayer, so must our loving attitudes toward each other be consistent! One secret of successful marriage, for example, is the continuous expression of love.

Is my love personal? A prime characteristic of true love is individuality. Jesus expressed His love at the cross to individual lost souls. Do I make my love personal? Only monogamous marriage can be the vehicle of true romantic love. "Mass production love" is meaningless. One must show a loved one that he is intimately concerned about her only. Christian marriage is such a close relationship that success is dependent on this individuation. On this premise comes the joy of giving to each other. Thus, the husband rejoices in giving to the wife and providing for her.

Do I allow love to feed my life? Am I "lovable" as I relate to a loved one? Am I the kind of person who elicits love in return? As I show concern to others, I will receive love. When I meet the real needs of people's lives, they will love me!

Love cannot be taken for granted. Love returned is love completed: "For God so loved the world that he gave his only begotten Son, that whosoever believeth in him should not perish, but have everlasting life" (John 3:16).

Young people contemplating marriage must believe this and live by it.

"Love knows no limit to its endurance, no end to its trust, no fading of its hope; it can outlast anything. It is, in fact, the one thing that still stands when all else has fallen!" (I Corinthians 13:7, 8, Phillips Translation).

THE MIRACLE OF MARRIAGE

Yet successful preparation for Christian marriage involves more than romantic love. Marriage is a difficult business — it is a serious business. To seek success in marriage without spiritual help and complete dedication is virtually impossible. Christian marriage is a miracle.

Americans do not appreciate the miracle of electricity as do people of other nations. Why? Because most of us deal with this wonder each hour of the day as we push buttons and pull switches. Many people who live in the mountains lose their appreciation for the miracle of God's handiwork and creative power. Those of us in the valley or on the plain must remind them of the wonders of the mountains. Even many Christians have lost their sense of awe at the conversion of a friend or relative — our world's greatest miracle! Why? Because we live so close to miracles that we get used to them.

Christian marriage is like this. We are tempted to be idealistic and teach that a Christian home is easy to establish and available to all. We take successful family life for granted — we forget that in these days tidal waves of opposition assail a Christian home.

Establishing a Christian home is impossible when only human resources are employed; this enterprise calls for the partnership of God. Founding, growing, and structuring a great Christian home is nothing short of a miracle in this world! Yet, we live so close to it that we fail to see the wonder of it. Then before long we do not take marriage seriously at all. In fact, we use it for the subject matter of our jokes.

Christian marriage would seem impossible if we did not see it happen. Suppose we knew nothing about the marriage of two people living in faithfulness together as husband and wife for "as long as they both shall live." Presume that we were unfamiliar with our high ideals of the Christian home. Then imagine that I propose to you that two people — relative strangers actually — be bound together in a simple service and attempt to live in this faithful relationship. Let's say that they are even of very different personalities; from different backgrounds; of varying economic levels; and in all other ways far from being alike.

If you did not already know that such a faithful relationship was workable and possible, you would laugh at me and insist that it would not work — you'd probably say, "Why, that's nothing short of a miracle." And you would be right.

Is it too much to expect from man? "Only God can make a man — only God can remake a man." Only with the help of God could a couple expect to succeed in this serious business of building a Christian home. Only God can take the raw materials of two personalities, a house, furnishings, friends and neighbors, and remake these into a Christian home.

Some will say that they know of families which are happy and moral and well-adjusted, yet not Christian. They have "borrowed" God's blueprint for a Christian home without giving the Lord the credit! They are attempting to perform miracles on their own power. They have the structure for it, but not the lifeblood. Miracles are in the hands of God. Man and woman, though bound together by love, still need a spiritual bond which only God can provide.

It is interesting how people are united when they focus their attention and endeavor on a single focal point. Thus, a Christian couple launching into matrimony together will feel closer to each other because of their common faith in God. Later their love for their children will be stronger when the children accept Christ. All of it is too big a thing for us — we must have God to help in this miracle of marriage.

Harmony grows by living together. As one sees the many facets of human personality and the eccentricities of people he wonders that we all get along as well as we do. Unless there is a spiritual love to lubricate the moving cogs of family living there is bound to be friction. Families that live together happily meet the popular threefold test: they work together; they play together; and they pray together.

Like many miracles, building a great Christian home is a long range process. Over a period of years of working and playing and praying the God-blessed institution evolves. There are multiplied instances of painting the house together, of planning the annual vacation as a group, of sharing in the duties of the household. All these build great Christian citizenship.

THOSE WHO DO NOT MARRY

Many young people date and even become engaged, yet never marry. Others enter into marriages which, because of death, separation, or divorce, cannot last. What about them? What about their family needs? Community and friends can provide wonderful help here. However, there is no better psychological and social substitute for a family than the church. The thesis of this discussion is that a church and church friends can become "the family" for these single adults.

Many single adults have assumed leadership positions in every area of life. Others work quietly and tactfully behind the scenes as followers in almost every area of living. These people have opportunities to fill strategic places of service for God and their fellow men.

Perhaps you know a man like Bill Elsey, for example. Bill is a single adult who, after finishing college, went into a small business. He was one of the most active men in the civic life of his community. He sponsored several youth groups in the town and made a contribution to the lives of the boys not only by his work but by his example.

It is in his church, however, that Bill renders his greatest service. He is one of those valuable church members who possess both maturity and youthful enthusiasm. The young people with whom he works are the most dedicated and useful the church has seen in a long time. In his position in life, he has more free time than do many church members with families, and he also has the ability to decide how he can best use his time. Because of this freedom, he has been able to serve untiringly in the Lord's work.

Perhaps you have in your own church a young woman like Berta Horn. Berta, like Bill, is bubbling over with enthusiasm and creative ideas. She also has a sincere, mature Christian faith.

Berta holds a number of responsible positions in the church and community. When there is a need for extra help in the office or for a substitute pianist or song leader, she is always ready to respond.

Berta is attractive to the children in the church, and they all love her. She also works with the Campfire Girls. At the same time, her maturity gives a feeling of confidence to the parents whose children she leads. She accepts her responsibility as a steward under God.

You may know many other single adults in your church and community. We shall discuss some of their needs which can be met by the church:

They must be wanted and needed. The needs of single adults are those which are natural for any group of adults — but they are sometimes more intense! These often involve the need for opportunities of personal expression and for social contacts. The church can provide an outlet for the satisfaction of both of these needs.

The single adult needs a sense of belonging to the group. During the early years of adulthood, many persons, especially those who are unmarried, may be faced with the temptation to align themselves with the wrong groups in order to find contacts which satisfy social needs.

Usually single adults fall into two categories with reference to church loyalty. One group includes those who completely estrange themselves from the church, having left it in their adolescent years and often not returning until middle adult life. The other group constitutes the single young adults who have remained faithful to the church during this period of life and usually assume positions of leadership. Many times those who have separated themselves from the church are simply seeking, among groups outside the church, to satisfy their social needs.

They should be creative and busy. Some single adults, because of their educational, vocational, and social development, are unusually creative and enthusiastic. Thus they can serve the church in outstanding ways, particularly in programming. Also, many of them are engaged in vocational or professional work which is definitely church-related.

In the church skills developed through secular work may be utilized in many ways. One single woman was counselor for the high school in a small city. She had extensive training in the field of counseling and guidance and was the only person in the town who was well qualified in the field. Her services were invaluable to the church in this area of dealing with young people. Frequently the pastor called on her for help in some of his pastoral counseling.

A certain man had been an outstanding sales representative in his community for a number of years. When his church launched its building program, this single adult was made chairman of the fund-raising campaign. His genuine enthusiasm and skill as a salesman were used in a remarkable way in serving the Lord. This man's willingness to devote countless hours of his time to the project was rewarded by the church's oversubscribing its goal.

There are many ways in which single adults have made unusual and significant contributions in their churches. A number of years ago a survey was made of young people, single and married, in the state of Missouri. The purpose was to determine the service they were rendering in local churches. In this study, it was found that a high percentage of the leadership in Sunday school was provided by this single adult group.

Most single young adults in a career or business are creative and enthusiastic, and their abilities need to be expressed. It is tragic when this expression is given to less worthy causes than the church.

They need to belong to the fellowship. Psychologists and sociologists consider each adult who has set up his own household as a family unit. This is true even if there are no other people living with him. Many single adults who are working away from home in professions and vocations and also, many who are in school, constitute such "families." Although they usually make friends with people in their work or their school groups, they also need the kind of social and spiritual fellowship a church provides.

Christ intended that this social unit of the family be supplemented by the contributions of the church family.[4] The young adult who is away from his parental home or lives in a large city especially needs the fellowship of a church. In times of crises, a church family can prove invaluable to a single adult.

Church members who are married can see to it that single adults are frequently invited into their homes. Participating in the Christian fellowship of family units will enrich the lives of single adults. Many times single adults can be a great inspiration to the children of a family in the church. They can provide ideals for young people in the church families.

Single adults can make a significant contribution as they serve on the various boards and committees of the church. In certain areas they may have had more experience and have more creative ideas than some of the married people in the church membership. Although it is not always true, many times the single adults in a church will have had more opportunities for formal education. Sometimes a single adult may be able to represent the church at associational meetings and conventions when a church member with a family would not be free to attend. Such activities draw single adults into the family circle of the church.

In conclusion, we have developed a place in our American society for the gradual preparation for those who marry. There is also a rich and fulfilling life opportunity for those who do not marry.

The home, community, church, and family must work together to prepare young people for these ways of life.

---

[4] M. D. Hugen, *The Church's Ministry to the Older Unmarried* (Grand Rapids: Eerdman's, 1959). Dr. Hugen gives an interesting discussion of this koinonia-activity in his book.

2. The Honeymoon and the First Months

". . . duologue of love"

WHERE DIALOGUE BEGAN in these formative years, now a real duologue of love is matured in the first days and months of marriage. The new, intimate communication and unification of two committed persons builds toward common grounds of dialogue and understanding. This begins with our traditional and initial experience called the "honeymoon."

Although many world cultures have a post-marriage period comparable to our honeymoon, few have dramatized and romanticized it. Too much emphasis has been placed on the honeymoon here in our contemporary, Western civilization. Yet, it should not, however, be minimized.

The beginning of a marriage has the psychological import of other beginnings. A wholesome preparation (and anticipation) for the first days of the marriage relationship is good.

Nevertheless, some harmful ideas have entered into our traditional concept of the honeymoon: (1) It is an artificial period of life. We have thought of it as a cloistered period of utopian bliss. This is artificial and unrealistic. Though the honeymoon ought to be as nearly an ideal setting as possible (and one ought to expend considerable funds and make thorough arrangements so that it has the environment for happiness) it ought not become a fetish. As one expert suggests, "The honeymoon ought to go on for years and years . . ." What we call the honeymoon is only the beginning of a new relationship. Therefore, if it is too artificial, it will not serve its proper purpose. The couple ought to have some social contacts with other people during these days of honeymoon and they ought to be involved in activities together other than the intimate contacts of marriage.

(2) Another harmful aspect of the honeymoon is that it may involve so much travel and activity that real conversation is limited. The honeymoon ought to be a time for new dialogue — a dialogue of love. Although the intimacy of the honeymoon will probably minimize verbal contact, conversation ought to be a real part of the honeymoon. The climate under which the two people live ought to give opportunity for a new kind of verbal communication. This will call for some honest frank discussion which probes even deeper into personality, prejudices, and feelings than the serious pre-marriage conversation did.

(3) The honeymoon is a "testing time" for the marriage. Here is another wrong idea. This has not only been a false, but a very dangerous concept. Many times the happiest marriages come out of the most disillusioning honeymoons. Also, a perfect adjustment in the artificial and brief atmosphere of the honeymoon does not guarantee a long range happiness in married life. Sometimes the adjustments involved in the honeymoon will simply be the continuing ones which were begun during the engagement. Thus, though it may not be the happiest time, it may be a very valuable time and make married life after the honeymoon more successful.

(4) The honeymoon is a status symbol — another harm-

ful idea. The place, length, and circumstances of the honeymoon should be chosen on the basis of the honest interest of the bride and groom. The honeymoon has become a social issue in our society. This detracts from the real value of the experience. The couple should go to a place and do things which are personally satisfying to them both. In this kind of emotional climate they will find the best adjustment. If, however, they go abroad or to some famous honeymoon place and do things which honestly bore them, just to conform, the whole point of the honeymoon experience is wrong. In other words, if a young couple has no interest in going abroad for a honeymoon, they ought not do so just for the sake of the social columns in the local newspaper.

(5) Another misleading viewpoint is that the honeymoon is not related to marriage. The honeymoon ought to be a good transition into settled married life. That is, there ought not to be too much of an abrupt change between the two since this will make the first days and weeks of being "at home" rather disillusioning. By contrast, the responsibilities of getting back to one's work and establishing the home might seem like drudgery — this would be unfortunate. Therefore, an overly spectacular honeymoon may create some psychological problems because of the comparisons involved with real life later.

Additional suggestions could be added to the above but the statements are sufficient to indicate that the protocol for the modern honeymoon is in evolution and perhaps ought to be re-evaluated constantly.

FACING MARRIAGE REALISTICALLY

Wouldn't it be wonderful if every young married couple could actually live in the beautiful and perfect harmony with which the great romantic novels of fiction seem to end? From our childhood we have come to the last page of the great romances and have read the words, "and they lived happily ever after." This is, of course, an imaginary condition which a writer of fiction can easily manufacture.

One does not have to live long, however, to realize that even marriage, as other close friendships, is made up of imperfect human beings. Since the Garden of Eden man has had the imperfections of sin in his life. All human relationships — regardless of how wonderful they are — are imperfect relationships. No two persons are faultless enough to live together in the intimacy of marriage without some disharmony. So, in order for us to improve our own personal relationships with each other, we must realize that these relationships are between persons who are not perfect. Yet, the problems can be handled well if both marriage partners have a unifying Christian ideal.

Remember the godly homes of the Hebrews? Are most of our modern American homes as permanent and secure as those Jewish homes? Many cultural changes have taken place in recent years. Remember when our forefathers came to this country? They established great Christian homes much like those of Europe. They lived in large houses built for two or three generations. Spacious dining rooms and kitchens enabled them to read the family Bible together — and family devotions were a part of family living. Yet, in recent generations we are building smaller houses, and each generation lives unto itself. The family has disintegrated in its work and interests.

Also, we change houses and furniture so frequently that our children do not build up a sense of security and stability as they live in these changing homes. Added to this is the trend toward packing the old family Bible away! Thus we have broken down the traditional associations of Bible and Christ in the home; family life and devotional periods; and the "worship at the table."

We need a revival of the centrality of God in the home, in the Person of Christ — only then will we have security and permanency. This will enable us to "live happily ever after" and cause two imperfect persons to live in harmony.

There Are Activities Which Help

What are some things young people can do to cement their marriage — to help in a practical way during the early days of the relationship?

(1) Do things together. Work on the budget together; prepare Sunday school lessons together; shop together; and share in all things.

(2) Read the Bible and pray together. Husband and wife should talk openly about individual spiritual problems.

(3) Go out to dine together. They should be sure to take their annual vacation together and spend time together socially. Individual social and recreational life is good but must be kept secondary.

(4) Always go to church together. Separate church attendance always harms this spirit of unity and understanding in marriage, aside from the spiritual disintegration it causes.

(5) Do some worthwhile Christian tasks together such as a community mission project or helping some person in need.

(6) Make sacrifices for each other — this deepens any relationship. Make these regularly and consistently.

All of these things prepare the soil so that the Holy Spirit can perform a miracle in marriage.

There was a lost tribe in Africa which had a most unusual custom. When a young man and woman were united in tribal marriage, their wrists were pricked and as blood came forth, the priest rubbed their wrists together and mingled the blood. This portrayed, to the tribe, their unity — they were one blood for life. This serves as a meager illustration of the spiritual unity of Christian marriage. How much more beautiful is the spiritual unity and confidence in Christian marriage?

Young couples must realize the seriousness of Christian marriage and the impossibility of its success without divine help. This unity and focus on the spiritual provides the best grounds for real deep conversation. Spiritual matters are the most important. Therefore, emphasis on them causes serious, growing dialogue.

GROWING IN CONVERSATION

In his book, *Sex Facts and Fiction for Teenagers,* Eugene B. Mozes, M.D., gives discussion on each of these "common grounds" for compatability in marriage: common interests, temperament, companionship, common background, adaptability, and age. Good dialogue at the time of marriage grows out of a satisfaction of these factors. Thus, dialogue helps relationships (as we have seen all along) but relationships also encourage or discourage dialogue! The vocation of every newly married person is to enter into dialogue with the marriage partner.

Reuel L. Howe lists the characteristics of this person. He says:

1. The dialogical person is a total, authentic person.
2. The dialogical person is an open person.
3. The dialogical person is a disciplined person.
4. The dialogical person is a related person.[1]

The application of these four characteristics gives clarity to our concept of the newly married person in conversation. He is "total, open, disciplined, and well-related." This constitutes a rather good analysis of maturity. The bride and groom should have paid the price of maturity — this is really the foundation for rich, meaningful conversation. People who *face* life can *discuss* it!

[1] Reuel L. Howe, *The Miracle of Dialogue* (New York: Seabury Press, 1964), pp. 69-83.

Growing up is a natural process. Yet, maturing into a worthwhile and productive person costs a great price. The shrewd businessman knows that nothing in this world is really free (although some things "seem" to be free). Sooner or later, directly or indirectly, one pays the price for all commodities of life. Even Christ's salvation which is free to all in its availability, actually costs one's whole life in full surrender to Christ and His will!

The young man and woman who want a Christian home must pay a high price to secure it. A prominent college dean of women, now retired, recently stated that the sorrow of her career was the memory of hundreds of young women entering into marriage without an awareness of its cost. A young husband or wife must pay the price of communion with God in devotional life, moral living, choosing things under God's leadership, and bearing crosses, if he or she would reach true Christian maturity in family life.

Many experiences, joyous and sorrowful, paved the way for Moses to lead the children of Israel out of Egypt and through the wilderness ordeals. Righteous living, which is centered in God's will, always costs, and the wise person does not seek to avoid such costs. Building a life is like building a business or a bank account — it must be done consistently with serious investments every day!

Some psychiatrists today are suggesting that adults can solve their problems if they can do away with all guilt feelings. The Bible teaches that men are going a little too far in this theory. Although people ought not develop a morbid sense of guilt without doing something about it, they should, on the other hand, feel bad when they do wrong!

In fact, not to feel sorry for sin is a dangerous trend; it is not realistic. If we did rear a generation without a sense of wrongness and guilt about their sins, they would recognize no basis for morality or religion. They would be living in ivory towers, running away from life. Moreover, repentance would appear to be unnecessary, if not impossible. Rather than loss of guilt feelings, we need a revival of conscience and an awareness of the wickedness and awfulness of sin, the love of God for all sinners, and the power of Christ to atone for sins. When we substitute for the reality of sin a blind running away from life, we are lost.

Young married couples will make mistakes. They should feel guilty when they do. But their hope lies in honest conversation and forgiveness of each other. Then they can go, together, to God in prayer for His forgiveness — this cements a marriage.

LEARNING TO LIVE WITH LIFE

Are you ever tempted to think of the ideal life as one in which there are no problems or heartaches? Perhaps you are — for the enjoyment of ease and pleasure is a normal human experience. Many newly married couples live in this dream world.

Actually, however, problems and heartaches inevitably come into every life. One test of a person's emotional maturity is his ability to face up to life's difficult situations. Only sick people seek constantly to run from reality.

Bill Nelson is approaching his middle twenties and is doing well in the large corporation where he works. He performs a rather routine type of work which never demands too much of him. Lucy, his young wife, manages the household in a remarkable way. Everyone knows she is a capable person. She keeps the family budget, works out the annual income tax return, does all the banking, and, in short, makes most of the family's decisions. Bill is happy to have her take this initiative, because he doesn't like to cope with the decisions necessary in managing the home.

Bill and Lucy are active in church life, although Bill never accepts a position of leadership. When asked to accept an office in Sunday school, he usually gives as his reason for refusing the excuse that he is "too busy." His real reason is an unwillingness to confront the problems and responsibilities the job would require. Bill has never learned to make decisions.

Actually, Bill has lived for almost twenty-five years "in" this world without learning to live "with" it. As a child he depended on his parents to make decisions for him. When he reached his teens he followed the gang in whatever they did. Now as an adult, Bill Nelson still is afraid to live with life. He lets his young bride make the choices.

Bill has attempted to "ride free" without assuming the responsibilities God demands of all His mature, rational children. Bill has been a poor steward of his life this far. Fortunately, with God's help, he can learn to live in the family, if he will pay the price.

Thus, in summary, marriage ought not begin with "two strangers." Adjustments should have already been made during courtship and engagement. The honeymoon continues this adjustment (although it is accelerated) and should not be dramatized and over-idealized. Marriage should be faced realistically and problems should be faced together. What are some typical problems newly-weds face? Study these:

1. The problems that arise in leaving the life of a single person to take up the responsibilities of a married person.

2. Beginning a home on a different financial scale than that which either has been used to. Beginning a home with fewer material possessions than those in their parents' homes.

3. Problems arising in connection with a working wife. Should the husband do more house work? Should the wife get to spend what she earns?

4. Problems that arise in adjusting to the personal habits of each other, as: using the same toothpaste, dress, speech, closet, and others.

5. Relationships to in-laws who take an over-active inter-est in all matters concerning the family.

6. Problems arising over the matter of who shall control the purse strings. Overspending, not supporting the wife in the way her father did; or allowing the wife to work and help support the family are other related problems.

7. Problems arising from living in the husband's or wife's parental home.

8. The refusal of one partner to accept the friends of his or her mate.

9. The difference in the partners' "Philosophies of Life." Differences in religious beliefs and conflicts in religious ac-tivities are problem areas.

10. Failure on the part of the husband to continue to "court" his wife may cause her to have a cool attitude toward him. What are some ways a couple may keep their "young love" alive?

11. At what point in marital conflict should the couple seek help from a counselor? Who are some people who can give help when conflicts or problems arise in the home?

A spiritual permeation of everything is most important in these early days and months. Activities of sharing seal the relationship — as does open and frank conversation. This causes both parties to face issues, to handle guilt in healthy ways, and to learn to live with life realistically.

One might, in conclusion, say that:

1. Marriage is for emotionally mature adults regardless of chronological age.

2. True maturity, independence, freedom and happiness in marriage cannot be acquired by dollars, prestige, and power — nor does one just "grow into it."

3. This maturity comes when we produce more than we take in — then we are qualified for marriage. This is needed for the give and take of it!

A word should be added to this conclusion relative to

marriage and military service. Many young people are thus involved and need help today. This comment is necessarily brief, but may help clarify some of the issues.

1. *War marriages* are different from *marriage in war time* — effects also are different.

2. Extreme caution is needed in the anticipation of marriage during any period of crisis and stress such as war.

3. The ingredients of marriage and the home are the same, but the amount, timing, and courtship are different. The objectives, love, and understanding are about the same as in peace-time marriages.

4. It seems that sweethearts can wait more patiently than wives or husbands.

5. Couples who are engaged or married before a period of service should agree on their behavior *before* he or she leaves for service.

6. If "dating" is agreed on, it is best to limit it to "group without pairing" dating practices.

7. Absence may or *may not* make the heart grow fonder!

There is almost unlimited aid (counseling, financial, and social help) available to the young man or woman whose partner is involved in the military. Some are: World War II Veterans Benefits; Medical and Domiciliary Benefits (Veterans Administration); Vocational Rehabilitation Act; National Education Act and GI Bill; Disability Compensation; Disability Pension; Death Compensation and Pension (World War II Act); National Service Life Insurance; VA Guardian Service; Burial Benefits (Federal and State); and many new aids in the National Education Act of 1965.

Conclusion

The sacredness of marriage, according to the Judeo-Christian tradition, has three main features:

1. It is a "commitment," not just a "contract" — this includes spiritual faith.

2. It is public in character — a "profession before God and man."

3. It is the free acceptance of a bond — "self-control and sacrifice" is involved.

J. B. Phillips in his translation, *Letters to Young Churches,* gives the following as the thirteenth chapter of First Corinthians. Adapt it to the beginning love of Christian marriage.

> If I were to speak with the combined eloquence of men and angels I should stir men like a fanfare of trumpets or the crashing of cymbals, but unless I had love, I should do nothing more. If I had the gift of foretelling the future and had in my mind not only all human knowledge but the secrets of God, and if, in addition, I had the absolute faith which can move mountains, but had no love, I tell you I should amount to nothing at all. If I were to sell all my possessions to feed the hungry, and for my convictions, allowed my body to be burned, and yet had no love, I should achieve precisely nothing.
>
> This love of which I speak is slow to lose patience — it looks for a way of being constructive. It is not possessive: it is neither anxious to impress nor does it cherish inflated ideas of its own importance.
>
> When I was a little child I talked and felt and thought like a little child. Now that I am a man my childish speech and feeling and thought have no further significance for me.
>
> At present all we see is the baffling reflection of reality; we are like men looking at a landscape in a small mirror. The time will come when we shall see reality whole and face to face! At present all I know is a little fraction of the truth, but the time will come when I shall know it as fully as God now knows me!
>
> In this life we have three great lasting qualities — faith, hope, and love. But the greatest of them is love.

3. The Parent of the Child

*". . . non-verbal response, questions
and answers, and discourse"*

THIS VERY CENTRALITY of the child in the family may create
problem areas. God intended that the little world of the
home would be a learning and proving ground for life. What
parts do wise Christian parents play in the leadership of the
child in this world of the home? The following discussions
will attempt workable answers.

In this chapter we want to discuss, basically, the child
in the home, but to do this we will have to talk about several
things with reference to the changing home structure of our
day. Some things will be suggested that will be helpful both
to parents and to church workers with children. If in one
instance we refer to the principle or the idea involved from
the viewpoint of the parent, those readers who are church
workers with this age group will try to interpret the idea
with reference to their responsibility. If an example pertain-
ing to the church worker is given, those who are parents will
make the same transition or translation for themselves.

Three main factors are to be considered in this discussion.

43

Number one is the changing family pattern of our day. Number two, the changing idea of evangelism in the home. Number three, the changing concept of Christian guidance in the home.

THE CHANGING FAMILY PATTERN

The very idea of marriage changes life for two individuals. The adjustments involved here are many, as we have seen in the previous chapter. There are adjustments that come as two personalities enter into a new world — into a relationship that one could almost say is impossible. Remember that even those of Christ's day, when they heard about this Christian life (and thus by inference the concept of Christian marriage), said, "It sounds good, but it won't work." They didn't say it in those words, but this was the reception of the idea of Christian harmony, unity and faithfulness. And so, the standards are high, and the adjustments are many.

Let us look at some of the changing roles that are emerging in our day. First of all, the husband and wife roles are changing rapidly. Sometimes the husband wonders what his role really is in family life. A few years ago we were emphasizing the problems and advantages related to the working wife. We don't even bother to talk about that any more. Now we are talking about the newest problem related to the changing role of husband and wife — the moon-lighting job. Within a decade the average American married couple will probably hold down an average of three to four jobs. The tendency is that the primary vocational job of the husband will be reduced, probably, to a 30-hour week. Before long (and the tendency definitely follows), he will get a second job. This will make three jobs for the family if the wife is already working.

There are some sociologists and psychologists who believe that the pattern will progress even further. As women's vocational time is reduced, maybe some of the working wives

will get a second job. That will make four positions for just
two people. This has a great impact on the changing roles
of husband and wife. Already in many families, the wife
does the yard work and the husband pushes the buttons
which do the dishes and the laundry. This is not too unusual.

Sometimes our children must have to stop and say, "Now,
let's see — he's the daddy — no, she's — no, he's the daddy,
that's right." These various roles and tasks around the home,
which identified us in our roles as husband or wife, father or
mother, man or woman, are now becoming very confused.
This brings about a total change of pattern in the family.
It probably means that those of us who are interested in
family life from the Christian viewpoint must begin asserting ourselves in the established parental roles.

This implies that husbands who feel themselves slipping
out of the real father role are going to have to take some
conscious steps to re-positionize themselves before their wives
and children. Perhaps some men will want to take more
initiative in family devotion than they have been doing
in the past. Maybe some men will want to revert back to
activities and functions in family life which have traditionally
set them up as husband or fathers. Many of the wives and
mothers will consciously and purposefully make some changes
in the things they do and the way they dress. They will assume responsibilities in family life so as to again gain a fixed,
stereotyped role of wife and mother. We may have to arti-
ficiate, in other words, in order to get back to where we
should be. So it means that those of us who are Christians
and who are concerned about these strategic roles in the
family may have to do some conscious things to revive them.

And then, of course, when parental roles are confusing,
there come changes with reference to the child's position in
the family circle; and because of this, many children are
shifting in their own positions. They are not sure how they
should relate to father and to mother, because they are con-

fused about the parental roles even as the parents themselves are confused. In addition, we are just coming out of a period — a period of almost 19 years — where there has been a definite change in the position of the child in the family, anyway.

We are leaving the period of the "growing pains" of what we might call the "child-centered home." This began almost two decades ago relating to certain aspects of the progressive education movement. There were certain theories which young mothers took as acceptable with reference to nurturing a child. The theories centered around ideas like: if Johnny wants to swing on the draperies like Tarzan, we had better let Johnny swing, or we will impede the development of his personality. If Susie wants to jump on the glass-topped coffee table, we had better let her do it, or we will warp her development for all of life.

Later, certain child psychologists and educators who advocated certain viewpoints of this theory made some changes. Now we are in a kind of pendulum swing toward a better and happier medium as to the position of the child in the home. This has great implications not only for the family pattern (getting it back in focus again), but also in terms of our understanding of the spiritual development of the child. Where the child is over-centralized in the home the whole schedule and pattern of the family accommodates to the child. Then, the child does not learn his position in life and in the world. He cannot develop skills.

God's plan is that the youngster will be nurtured in a little world of the home, the neighborhood, the church, the community, in which he learns how to fit in — to a degree, at least. When all other influences accommodate to him, then he doesn't learn this.

But we are coming to a better, happier medium, and most parents and teachers understand now that the child is not to be central. The world does not accommodate to him. In fact, the little world of the family had better not, or he will

not learn how to adjust to other people and to life situations
— certainly not to spiritual relationships later on!

Also, the child's role is changing in the home in his relationship to other people. The home is no longer a tight cita-
del. It's a more expanding and fragmented thing. The child
has more interest in neighborhood and community. In fact,
by the time he gets into his mid-teens, the typical American
youngster has almost as many fringe interest and involve-
ments in the community as his parents do.

Recently the writer counseled with a sixteen-year-old girl.
The youngster was really in an emotional state; and after she
talked a while, I learned that she was an officer in seventeen
different clubs and organizations in community, school, and
church! It then became evident that her father and mother
were in the same situation.

Thus, the child doesn't have the security which he needs
in the tighter society of the home. This closeness, to which
he retreats after having gone out into his expanding world,
is what God intended the family to provide.

And so, this becomes another problem which probably
necessitates the father and mother re-evaluating their roles,
understanding what they represent to the child. The father
being the one who will present to the child security, an-
chorage, such as the image which Jesus used in His parallel
with the Heavenly Father. The mother again assumes her
role as the listener, the one who is ready; the one who is the
queen of the palace of the home, the one who is there and
available. Reassuming these roles definitely relates to the
child's sense of the home being a closely knit kind of a
world in which he can learn how to live, grow and develop.

A Changing Concept of Evangelism in the Home

Now we are beginning to understand the ways the child
learns living skills for the world right in his own home. We
are, therefore, learning that the home itself can become the

place in which the foundation is built for the child's relationship to God. God intended for the home to be the place (along with the church) in which the child would learn the skills and understandings and the maturity levels that would be necessary for his religious experiences later on.

For example, it is in the home that the child is supposed to learn sharing, a sense of responsibility, give and take, all of these things which are necessary to life and to spiritual experiences. The child is supposed to learn the idea of giving to the point of sacrifice, but if a child has lived in an over-centralized home where he doesn't go through experiences where he learns what it means to give, then he cannot understand. It isn't just learning the skill, but it is learning the concept or understanding behind the skill. How can a child understand Jesus' dying on the cross and giving himself for the child, if the child has never given up anything in his life, up to that point? And so, when the mother deals with the child in ways in which he is led to give up things willingly, she is laying the foundation for spiritual understandings later on.

Are you aware of the fact that when the young mother is eating her breakfast and the baby is in the high chair, the mother may open one of the greatest doors to that human life that will ever be opened? The mother may eat her cereal with delight. The child watches her; the child smiles and senses the satisfaction of the mother. If the mother takes a spoon of the cereal, which she is eating and enjoying, and gives it to the child, this simple act may be the first spark of understanding on the part of that child. The child sees what it means to give something you want for yourself. As the youngster grows, he will exercise this understanding and give up something that he likes. He will first give to his mother. And then later on he will give to his father; finally, to his sister or to his brother.

Every parent who takes advantage of this kind of human

interaction may be forming the foundation for that child's religious experiences. Sometime later the child will repeat the concept in giving himself to Christ — in receiving the gift of salvation.

Now take responsibility, for example. There finally comes a time in the life of the infant when he begins to sense that he is a separate person, entity, and being. So far as we know, the infant cannot separate himself from mother, parent or friend. He just merges with the other personalities around him. Yet, with the give and take, and the satisfaction of needs, the older infant finally comes to the place where he begins to comprehend his separateness. A level of awareness develops and he begins to see himself as an individual personality.

Remember the first time he dropped a rattle? You remember how you picked it up and gave it to him. There was not much response. He gurgled and cooed and then he threw it down again. Then you picked it up. And finally when you picked up that rattle and gave it back to the child, a little different response took place. He began to understand. Do you remember when he began to throw it down just to see you pick it up and hand it back to him? It irritated you, didn't it? And yet that was the beginning! He saw that he could not only respond to action, but cause it! Thus, he was separate from mother through that action. God was already beginning to plant in that soul the mental understanding of the fact that "Thou Art Separate." Self-responsibility began to grow.

Therefore, the preparation for the child's future relationship with Christ and the child's discipline are interdependent. If we are the right kind of parents and take the time, we'll enable the child to build these steps of understanding, and developmental tasks, so that when he comes to the time to make a spiritual decision, he'll have the background and the understanding. He can also exercise the skills and the tools for doing it. Remember the first time you led your little child to give up something he really wanted? And do you remember the simple satisfaction that little child had, the first time he made a sacrifice? This is typical in human experience. Usually we overlook it. But it becomes the keystone upon which the Holy Spirit works on that life, later. Giving of self to Jesus can take place. Thus the home is a laboratory; it's a place in which you and I have the opportunity and the responsibility of laying the foundation stones for evangelism.

A Changing Concept of Christian Guidance

Recently, a woman in a conference asked, "I have a three-year-old child; when should I start disciplining him?" (Of course, her definition of discipline is like yours — not just spanking or not spanking). The leader answered, "My dear, about three years ago." One wanted to say even more than three years ago! When you first knew you were going to be a mother, you should have started disciplining yourself and understanding what the relationship would mean when the child comes. It's like putting money in the bank when we invest in these formative years.

We, in this way, have a new idea of the parent as teacher. One parent said, "I constantly hear conflicting views about disciplining my child — what should I do?"

This is a question every parent faces and seeks to solve in his or her own way. Some leaders in education and child care have, in the past, led us to feel that a child was reared best without discipline — physical or psychological. We were told that if we punished our children they would be harmed for life and that their personalities would be affected permanently. Others advised us that to "spare the rod" was to spoil the child. The educators first advocated free expression without love, but now we realize we need discipline with love!

Then another question comes to mind, "Should my Christian ideas about life have anything to do with the way I rear my children?" Let's look at these things and find a way of child care that is both wise, as far as science is concerned, and also good from the Christian point of view. First, however, I think we need to remind ourselves that these general suggestions may vary because of individual differences of children. Also, one's relationships with his children are constantly changing. At certain times I'll need to exert more control over my children than at other times. Also, I must remind myself constantly that one never solves all the problems, because they are constantly changing — that is, as we solve one, others are already arising. We all experience this in our own lives.

Because of the trend which suggests that we never discipline a child, we find some children "ruling" their families. This we have called the "child-centered home." This is the first time in history that man has placed so much importance on the child. Several causes are evident. One is the case of the parents who are simply too lazy or busy to pay much attention to the child and find it easier to let him always have his way. Some parents are too immature themselves, they were not taught respect in their own homes, there is lack of concern for property, and downright neglect for the children. Showing off a child has had its ill effects (logically this should come later when you've made something of him!) Children with these environments will likely have these characteristics:

1. Self-centered or bullying
2. Unconscious of the rights of others
3. Over-independent (they have not learned to be guided by others)
4. Messy, inefficient, and irresponsible in the care of personal things (it is easier to put the toy away yourself,

but better for the child to teach him to carry it to his
own toy box)

5. Unable to work with or under other people
6. Not responsive to God's demand of humility, convic-
    tion of sin, and moral discipline
7. Lack of concern for the welfare of other people

This type of home life gives Junior too much freedom because it is thought that to correct or discipline will inhibit
Junior's little personality! This is, of course, more harmful
to the child because he never learns to take orders, respect
property, or work in a team relationship.

The child is meant to be secondary in home life activities.
He needs to learn to "fit in"!

Later we shall think about the spiritual ideas involved in
the child-centered home.

On the other hand, constant and unreasonable discipline
is both un-Christian and harmful to the child. This may result in fitting the child into the cultural pattern "prescribed
for him." One good rule to remember is that the punishment or reward ought to relate to the evil or good behavior
causing it. This rule, however, cannot be used with very
young children who cannot understand.

For example, if the child will not allow the parent to prepare him to go out, then the punishment might be that he
would not be allowed the pleasure of going out. It is not
good to bribe with a money reward for high grades (in the
case of an older child) but the parent can explain that the
reward is in a sum of money placed in the fund for the
child's college education. In both these cases the punishment and the reward logically relates to the total learning
situation.

Any discipline which is just punishment for punishment's
sake is really over-discipline. Incidentally, much of this is
done when the parent is angry at the child and this again
is very dangerous.

One might sum it all up by saying that the right discipline will also serve the purpose of being a teaching method. We find discipline problems all through life. Problems in adolescence and adulthood stem from the same basic causes.

Also, discipline ought to be relaxed enough that parents can really enjoy children. Parents do not have to always understand their children. They often ask, "What is a boy?" or "What is a girl?" Look at Alan Beck's evaluations:

"Between the innocence of babyhood and the dignity of manhood we find a delightful creature called a boy. Boys come in assorted sizes, weights, and colors, but all boys have the same creed: To enjoy every second of every minute of every hour of every day and to protest with noise (their only weapon) when their last minute is finished and the adult males pack them off to bed at night.

"Boys are found everywhere — on top of, underneath, inside of, climbing on, swinging from, running around, or jumping to. Mothers love them, little girls hate them, older sisters and brothers tolerate them, adults ignore them, and Heaven protects them. A boy is Truth with dirt on its face, Beauty with a cut on its finger, Wisdom with bubble gum in its hair, and the Hope of the future with a frog in its pocket.

"When you are busy, a boy is an inconsiderate, bothersome, intruding jangle of noise. When you want him to make a good impression, his brain turns to jelly or else he becomes a savage, sadistic, jungle creature bent on destroying the world and himself with it.

"A boy is a composite — he has the appetite of a horse, the digestion of a sword swallower, the energy of a pocket-size atomic bomb, the curiosity of a cat, the lungs of a dictator, the imagination of a Paul Bunyan, the shyness of a violet, the audacity of a steel trap, the enthusiasm of a fire cracker, and when he makes something he has five thumbs on each hand.

"He likes ice cream, knives, saws, Christmas, comic books,

the boy across the street, woods, water (in its natural habitat), large animals, Dad, trains, Saturday mornings, and fire engines. He is not much for Sunday School, company, schools, books without pictures, music lessons, neckties, barbers, girls, overcoats, adults or bedtime.

"Nobody else is so early to rise, or so late to supper. Nobody else gets so much fun out of trees, dogs, and breezes. Nobody else can cram into one pocket a rusty knife, a half-eaten apple, 3 feet of string, an empty Bull Durham sack, 2 gum drops, 6 cents, a sling shot, a chunk of unknown substance, and a genuine super-sonic code ring with a secret compartment.

"A boy is a magical creature — you can lock him out of your workshop, but you can't lock him out of your heart. You can get him out of your study, but you can't get him out of your mind. Might as well give up — he is your captor, your jailer, your boss, and your master—a freckled-face, pint-sized, cat-chasing, bundle of noise. But when you come home at night with only the shattered pieces of your hopes and dreams, he can mend them like new with the two magic words — 'Hi, Dad!' "

"Little girls are the nicest things that happen to people. They are born with a little bit of angel-shine about them and though it wears thin sometimes, there is always enough left to lasso your heart — even when they are sitting in the mud, or crying temperamental tears, or parading up the street in mother's best clothes.

"A little girl can be sweeter (and badder) oftener than anyone else in the world. She can jitter around, and stomp, and make funny noises that frazzle your nerves, yet just when you open your mouth, she stands there demure with that special look in her eyes. A girl is Innocence playing in the mud, Beauty standing on its head, and Motherhood dragging a doll by the foot.

"Girls are available in five colors — black, white, red, yellow, or brown — yet Mother Nature always manages to select your favorite color when you place your order. They disprove the law of supply and demand — there are millions of little girls, but each is as precious as rubies.

"God borrows from many creatures to make a little girl. He uses the song of a bird, the squeal of a pig, the stubbornness of a mule, the antics of a monkey, the spryness of a grasshopper, the curiosity of a cat, the speed of a gazelle, the slyness of a fox, the softness of a kitten, and to top it all off He adds the mysterious mind of a woman.

"A little girl likes new shoes, party dresses, small animals, first grade, noise makers, the girl next door, dolls, make-believe, dancing lessons, ice cream, kitchens, coloring books, make-up, cans of water, going visiting, tea parties, and one boy. She doesn't care so much for visitors, boys in general, large dogs, hand-me-downs, straight chairs, vegetables, snow suits, or staying in the front yard. She is loudest when you are thinking, the prettiest when she has provoked you, the busiest at bedtime, the quietest when you want to show her off, and the most flirtatious when she absolutely must not get the best of you again.

"Who else can cause you more grief, joy, irritation, satisfaction, embarrassment, and genuine delight than this combination of Eve, Salome, and Florence Nightingale? She can muss up your home, your hair, and your dignity — spend your money, your time, and your temper — then just when your patience is ready to crack, her sunshine peeks through and you've lost again.

"Yes, she is a nerve-racking nuisance, just a noisy bundle of mischief. But when your dreams tumble down and the world is a mess — when it seems you are pretty much of a fool after all — she can make you a king when she climbs on your knee and whispers, 'I love you best of all!' "[1]

[1] Alan Beck, *What Is a Boy? What Is a Girl?* (New England Mutual Life Insurance Company, 1950).

READINESS FOR RELIGIOUS EXPERIENCES

This guidance geared toward a religious experience or the conversion of the child is becoming increasingly evident to Christian parents. The average age of conversion in many groups is in these years directly following the primary years. Some children make this important decision while they are primaries. The deep concern of every conscientious parent and leader is to make certain that the experiences their children have as primaries will help to prepare them to make this decision. How can a leader know when a child is ready? What experiences are necessary before a child is ready to make this decision? What influences a child's readiness? Some of these have just been seen. Application might be as follows.

Some concept of personal independence is essential to the experience of trusting Jesus as Saviour. This experience is a personal one. No one can take this step for another. Only when a child has developed enough personal independence to recognize that he can make an important decision independently is he ready for this religious experience.

A child grows in independence when he is encouraged to do for himself. Language development particularly helps the growing child to express his independence. When a child is able to express himself rather fully through the vehicle of language, he is aided tremendously in his search for independence.

Contacts with other children of his own age seem to enable him not only to be aware of his independence but to exercise it. As he gets into the play group, he begins to experience give and take and to see that other children of his level can exert influence also. His independence grows rapidly when he gets into the social play group. This development reaches a high level during the younger years. Another evidence of independence is in the assumption of responsibilities. The young child is usually eager to assume responsibilities although he does not often carry them out to the fullest. But in assuming them for a brief period of time he builds up his self-concept. A child who is never called on to assume responsibilities in family living and in church and school experiences will probably be retarded in the development of independence. This implies not only the assumption of responsibility for activities but also the assumption of responsibility for decisions.

The kind of human relationships which will build understanding of the child's relationship with God are necessary. The child's initial comprehension of all relationships begins at the human level. Home and church serve as schools for his skills and also as sources of content material. Dr. Harry C. Munro uses a phrase in this relationship, "the church, a school in Christian living." The implication here is that the church gives the child not only content but also working skills.

As the child builds social skills on the human level, he can begin to build an understanding of divine relationships. For example, experience of loving God comes out of the child's understanding of parental love (or parental substitute love). It enlarges and expands through contacts with other people and finally relates to God. It is as parents and teachers that we first give the child ways of experiencing love. From these he translates behavior and content into his relationships with God. Gradually, the child acquires an understanding of his relationship with God.

This is true of other concepts, too. His understanding of Jesus as his "best friend" is based on his experience with friends day by day. His understanding of God's forgiveness must be based on human experiences of forgiving and being forgiven.

A child whose home situation consists of poor personal relationships has difficulty in developing right concepts of

God. The parent or leader has opportunity to help these children, and she may give the child substitute experiences which will aid in the development of right concepts.

Some knowledge of the Bible is necessary. The child must have a rudimentary knowledge of Bible truths. Basic knowledge of what God has done, what Jesus did, the kind of behavior that pleases God, and how God takes care of people and some knowledge of what the Bible teaches about heaven and hell are necessary for the conversion experience. Of course, knowledge of Bible words is not essential to salvation, and the child does not have to be able to read. The Bible *truths* must be interpreted to him by adults.

As this understanding increases, the way is prepared for the conversion experience in the life of the child. From the standpoint of human activities the child must have reached a readiness level for conversion. In other words, he must have some opinion of himself and must have matured to the level where these things are evident:

1. He must have the intellectual ability to make conscious decisions with an understanding of the consequence of these decisions. In church life we call this psychological level "the age of accountability."

2. With this developing age of accountability there must be a sense of right and wrong, to the extent of feeling sorry for wrongdoing The child must be mature enough to have a feeling of guilt when he does things which he knows are against God's will. Theologically, this is called a state of conviction of sin. One would not require that the child have a deep understanding of all the ethical implications of guilt and wrong. But he must at least feel sorry for his wrongdoing and understand that sin is disobeying God.

3. He needs comprehension of the experience of giving to the extent of personal commitment. Here again the child's understanding of the giving of himself must be to the extremity of what we call commitment. He must understand

that it is a total giving and it is a giving because of personal desire.

4. He must have some experience with "identification" to accept Christ's vicarious sacrifice. If the child has not developed in his self-understanding to the level that he can project himself by identification into the role and life of someone else, he would be missing an essential tool of salvation. To be saved, a person must accept that sacrifice of Christ. If the child is not mature enough to understand this simple transaction, he will be limited in his understanding of salvation.

5. Some understanding of time-space relations is essential. Most churches would hesitate to accept for baptism and church membership a child who did not have some understanding of the concept of eternal life with God.

When the child has developed these abilities, he has the tools — from the human standpoint — to experience conversion. Only then can the Holy Spirit bring salvation to a child.

Building Your Child's Self-Confidence for a Real World

Having discussed the child's family pattern, discipline, and spiritual development, we now ask, "Does my child evidence confidence for life in a difficult world?" He has been prepared for and has experienced redemption; now how does he mature? Confidence comes from the child's having a good opinion of himself — this is a big part of maturity. One cannot overestimate the value of this self-evaluation even for the very young. The child gains confidence by being allowed to assume responsibility and do things in which he feels secure over and over again. Then, too, his self-confidence is enhanced by living with parents who by every action show that they are mature, settled, and confident in the way they live. Young children easily sense insecurity on the part of their parents.

First, let us look at this self-confidence of the child as it is built on his growing opinion of himself. The child's "self" may be defined as the individual as he is known to himself within the context of all his relationships. It is evident that this is a social definition of self. As the child's understanding of himself as a separate living creature emerges, he learns to have regard for himself. At an early age he learns to give and take simple objects which he either likes or dislikes. He is able to repeat behavior which is satisfying to him and this builds self-esteem as well as good relationships with others. Therefore, it can already be seen that the young child's self-confidence grows along with the emerging self. As he enters into later childhood, he will have a well formulated opinion of himself. During the first three years of his life this concept is very vague, no doubt.

How to Build Self-Confidence

In building the child's self-confidence the parent can provide six helps.

1. Social situations in the environment of the child which will call on his responses and actions. This will include the satisfaction of basic life needs. If he feels he has some part—along with his parents — in helping to supply his needs, he is already building self-confidence.

2. What his parents lead him to think of them. This will reflect on his mind what he thinks of himself.

3. The play activities of the child in the home, neighborhood, and church will broaden his concepts of his world. When this takes place, he is bound to have new conclusions about himself. For example, in his group he will draw concepts of his individual differences and begin to see his playmates as separate personalities apart from himself.

4. The child's physical health conditions his self-opinion particularly. This is considered by authorities to be true when the child, because of poor health conditions, has been

catered to by parents and thus becomes over dependent. When he is in good health and is able to help take care of himself, he gains the needed prestige and security. It is interesting to note that this is one of the first areas in life where the young child does begin to assume some responsibility for himself. When he and his mother are at the task of making him clean, he first understands that there is the possibility that he could be dirty. This otherness — separate from himself — helps him see himself as a clean individual and thus separate from some others.

5. Parents can build self-confidence in a child by seeing that there is a scarcity of strong emotional tensions within the family circle. If this is true, he will soon positionize himself as the aggressor or as the overly-passive participant in family activities. Involved in such social and emotional expression on the part of the child is the child's formation of definite opinions about himself.

6. A sixth method is to demand of him certain responsibilities in the family circle. Where he is the center and everyone caters to him his environment seems to merge with his own personality and he never discovers his separateness. On the contrary where the child has to fit into certain situations and is wisely disciplined he understands the give and take of life. Thus he sees himself as a separate individual.

When the child is drawn out as mentioned above, he will develop these good characteristics which are a part of his self-opinion: self-confidence, objective self-criticism, self-respect, self-acceptance, and motivation from within — this helps the child to understand that he can initiate influences in his environment. It will be noticed that all of the above means of regulating the child's environment for development of his confidence have a social aspect. Thus, one cannot over-emphasize the part of the parents in this teaching situation.

How to Draw Out a Child

During his early years a young child often goes through a period of negativism. He does not want to respond to others. This period may retard his development of self-confidence unless the parents deal with him wisely. They need to draw out his personality and be patient during this phase of his life. There are some things which will encourage the child along this line. They are:

1. Approval and acceptance by adults which give the child satisfactions. This approval makes him willing to be influenced continually by the opinion of adults in his environment. He really wants to be recognized as a person but doesn't yet know how to go about it.

2. Repetition of this recognition will help draw him out. He must be called on consistently to do certain things and respond in certain ways.

3. Security. Most child psychologists agree that the child is searching basically for security. As soon as a degree of security is felt by the child he is then anxious to project himself. It is the same idea as having a strong home base before one branches out. Therefore security, as an incentive, leads the child to understand himself as a person separate from others.

4. Challenge through experience that is stimulating. People who work constantly with the young find that the more children go through a satisfying experience the more often they want to do the same thing. There is a short attention span for these youngsters and the desire to repeat must be exercised regularly.

5. The rewarding of such achievement. Children need to be rewarded immediately after they have done something which is acceptable. This is a good rule to remember in all child relationships. Many parents make rewards too competitive instead of giving them as immediate and natural outcomes of some achievement in behavior.

Thus, as the young child has been drawn out repeatedly and led to do new things he goes through the human experience of overcoming a problem and coming out victoriously. An adult knows that when he has repeated experiences like this he begins to mature and build self-confidence. What is more edifying to the human personality of any age than to go through difficulty, come out victorious, and be able to know that one has done so?

PREPARING FOR CONFIDENCE IN GOD

The self-confidence of any human being emerges rapidly when he comes into contact with Divine Power. That is why one can see a rapid growth in self-realization on the part of an older child when he really comprehends his relationship with God. As discussed before in the earlier years — one through three — we are laying the foundation and fertilizing the soil for such later understanding and fulfillment. Let us do our best as parents to guide our children to real life experiences which will enable them to understand themselves better. We must not over protect them but discipline them in an atmosphere of love and affection; for only as they fit into a real world do they understand their role.

In conclusion, we can provide all of these stimulations in the environment to help crystallize this self-confidence, but the child finds it most complete when he gains confidence in the fact that God is on his side. Let us all work and pray to this end.

4. The Parent of the Teen-ager

". . . communication — not investigation"

The Boy was reared in Nazareth,
(As pure in heart as angel breath,
Chaste as the smile that lights God's face)
Played in its friendly market-place.
His parents gave him tender care,
A home of faith and love and prayer.
— JOHN F. HERGET

WE ARE GOING to take a strange journey through the mysterious no man's land of adolescence. Leaving from a point of departure, we are taking a journey and we hope to end at a destination. We will consider some wrong philosophies about adolescence. Some conclusions about these will be made for your guidance, as Christian parents and church leaders, of these young people.

In our day and age, when we are talking about adolescence, we are referring to a much longer age span than we used to. We used to think about adolescence as going from the twelfth through the eighteenth year. Then the scholars shifted gears and made more studies and said that it really ought to go through the twenty-first year. The most reputable psychologists and sociologists today consider adolescence to be the twelfth through the twenty-fourth year. One new idea reverts back to eighteen as the terminal year. Yet, probably the most accepted proposition indicates that adulthood begins with the twenty-fifth year. So this gives us a newer idea of this developmental period which we call "adolescence."

A *primary background idea is that adolescence is simply a natural, God-given period of human development.* It is failure to understand this that causes our wrong understandings and wrong philosophies of adolescence.

If you were to go to your city library and study the stacks of books and pick out the psychology and the secondary education books of a generation ago, you would find in most of them that the specialists, even the scholars of that period, looked upon this period which we call adolescence as a mysterious period of life. You and I are the products of this kind of teaching. It is not unusual at all for parents (as their children approach their teens) to say, "I'd like to take a ten-year vacation."

For example, a member of the nominating committee goes to enlist a Sunday school teacher. She starts out by saying that she represents the nominating committee of the church; that after prayer and consideration they have sought God's will and have concluded as a group that the person being interviewed is the one who ought to teach the Sunday school class. People are depending upon the prospect. God depends upon him. There are great rewards in teaching God's Word. There are personal satisfactions in being able to nurture Christians, and so forth. This representative makes the wise, good appeal.

The person being interviewed listens to the appeal and nods, and is in a receptive mood. He agrees with the person representing the committee in terms of all these things mentioned, and is just about ready to accept when he stops and asks, "By the way, Mrs. Jones, what age group was it that they wanted me to teach?" And Mrs. Jones, representing the nominating committee, hesitates, flushes a little, stammers and finally says, "Well, we wanted you to teach intermediates." And the response of the person being enlisted is very typically this, "Oh — no!! Give me the kids, give me the old folks, but not the young people."

And out of this kind of false psychology — this false understanding of what adolescence really is — we have built up a tremendous fear. We see the adolescent as a man from Mars. Actually, this is just one of several periods of development in the human life span.

Life is a gradual, unfolding process and as Havighurst says, "Each stage must be built on the prior one." This is God's plan. No period is any more mysterious than any other period of development. There are several stages of human development, much like adolescence. However, you don't find much emphasis on them in written works. We define adolescence as the period in which the person is leaving childhood and entering adulthood. And we say that it's this dual phasing that makes it so mysterious; he's a child one moment and an adult the next.

But this is not the only such period in life. There is what we might call the "first adolescence." It comes (and elementary workers know this) when the human personality is leaving infancy and entering childhood. Remember that youngsters of yours back at the age of 18 to 36 months? He went through a shy period and you just wanted to disown him. You'd say, "Meet Aunt Susie," and he'd say, "No!" Remember he sometimes acted absolutely infantile; the next minute he acted rather like a mature child? That was the "first adolescence." And yet you didn't say, "Oh, I just don't want to deal with a child during that period. I just can't understand him. I don't want to have anything to do with him."

The main changing period we think about, however, is what we call the change of life. When the human personality is leaving young adulthood and entering middle adulthood there are many problems and many syndromes of behavior that are difficult to understand. Yet, we still see him or her as a human being and try to understand him.

Then there is still another period of overlapping characteristics. That is when one leaves adulthood and enters senescence. Grandma does some crazy things. But we try to deal with her; we try to understand why she does these things.

But somehow we have picked out this one period, adolescence, and we have said, "Teen-agers are different." Because of this false premise, many of the ways in which we have dealt with young people have been false. Naturally, when you form your tools upon a false idea, they are going to be wrong tools.

Thus, the first thing is to accept adolescence as this normal, human developmental period of life—God-given. There is nothing weird about it at all. These stages are all necessary; one builds upon another. And so, if we would really understand these young people and have a good foundation upon which to deal with them, we must first accept them as healthy human beings, going through a natural period of development.

The second background principle is that adolescents are going through a period of development in which they are finding their own way. Let's say that we have another false philosophy. That is, if we would deal with teen-agers and adolescents as we ought, we think we must first understand them. Too often we attempt to understand them by finding out from them why they do that which they do. This is a false philosophy.

The problem is that the adolescent doesn't know why he is doing what he is doing. And here again, many of our methods of dealing with him have been to no avail because they have been built upon this wrong thesis. Too many parents of teen-agers go around with one eye shaped like a keyhole. They become detectives and this is wrong.

A better example is this. A junior high school girl comes home from school. The front door of the house opens, and she is crying. She throws the books on the hall table and runs up the stairs, wailing and sobbing. The mother hears her bedroom door slam. She hears the weight of her daughter's body as she sinks on the bed, and the tears roll. She's a wise mother and she waits a little while. Finally she goes up and she knocks on the door and gets permission to enter her daughter's room. Then she goes in and sits down on the edge of the bed by her daughter and says, "Honey, can mother help?" Or she says, "Honey, Mom's here — if you need her."

Now if she's an unwise mother, what will she do? She'll go up and barge in the room and she'll start: "Why? Why are you doing this?" But you see the joke is on this mother. Mary doesn't even know "why" herself. Mary says, "Mom, I wish I knew. I don't know myself. Something happened at school. I just don't know."

Mary was trying to leave the known land of childhood and go through this no man's land of adolescence. Though she has some remote ideas and a rough road map, she really has to find her way as you and I did, by trial and error. How did the adolescent of yesterday find his way through the wilderness of adolescence? By trial and error, chiefly.

Then, there is symbolism involved. There is a great deal of symbolism in what represents childhood and that which represents adulthood to the teen-ager. Perhaps Mary tried something at school that day which represented adulthood, but she made a fool out of herself. It upset her equilibrium and she became frustrated and ran home crying. She can't define the situation.

When, for example, your teen-ager acts like she doesn't love you any more or when she turns on you, something happened which caused her temporarily to associate you with childhood. Something you did, something she thought you did, or something that you just temporarily represented to her was involved. And therefore, in this search all she needed to do was to divorce herself temporarily from you. You represented that childhood which she's supposed to be leaving. She doesn't quite know how, but she's supposed to. And many a parent becomes troubled when a son or daughter in this age bracket seems to turn against them completely for a while. They must be understanding. This rejection doesn't mean he or she doesn't love you anymore — it just means that you have been associated with something that represents childhood.

Then, too, there will be some things, which, for the teen-ager, represent adulthood. It may be a practice his peer group carries on. And some of the things that symbolically represent adulthood to the teen-ager are illogical. These things are just as immature as they can be, but that's not the point. Symbolism isn't necessarily logical. Yet, it represents adulthood. This is what confuses parents and causes worry.

Yet, for the adolescent to align himself with others who are taking the same journey toward adulthood, satisfies him. For example, we went through a period a few years ago where the status symbol, the image of leaving childhood and entering adulthood for teen-agers in America, had to do with conformity or non-conformity. For a period there, conformity became the symbol of teen-agers of childhood. To conform was to be childlike. Non-conformity became the symbol, to the teen-ager, of adulthood. This was supposed to be his objective.

One of the most dynamic developments which came out of this period of teen-ager symbolism was the beatnik movement — the break with conformity. These youngsters divorced themselves symbolically from conformity. Mom was conformity; dad was conformity; the church was conformity; all rules represented conformity. Dressing like everyone else was conformity; eating when you were supposed to eat was conformity. Conformity represented childhood. Remember, all which represents childhood is to be left by them. Yet, they didn't know which way to go. So "non-conformity," or the beatnik approach, became the symbol for getting away from it all. However, when they got in the beatnik movement, it was conformity personified. You had to eat aspirin whether you liked it or not. You had to read poems you didn't understand. That's why the fad didn't last. All of this proved it's just symbolic.[1]

Perhaps your youngster is going through a phase in which he associates going to church, Sunday school, or reading the Bible with childhood. During this period Sunday school is childish. This association with childhood causes him to estrange himself from it. This disturbs some of us and we say, "Oh, he has lost his faith." He'll be back in a little while.

And so, it isn't important to find out from teen-agers why they behave in a certain way. Half the time they don't know. Rather, one must *be there when they need you!* And though it may not seem possible to you, as a parent, you can help them through this no man's land. You will (symbolically) represent security and consistency.

Sometimes this estrangement from family and church continues, but usually it is temporary. Several years ago there was a study made of the loss of young people from the church. Most of them, the study showed, eventually come back. There is the great problem of preoccupation during the teens; most young people drop out of church life simply because of preoccupation. They become preoccupied with other things: romance, getting married, having children, and getting started in business. When this strong preoccupation diminishes they usually come back to the church.

The danger is that we will assume the parental role of de-

[1] Ruth Strang, *The Adolescent Views Himself* (New York: McGraw-Hill Book Company, Inc., 1957), pp. 83-128.

tective. We pry — even though our objectives are worthy. We say, "Son, I only want to know why you are doing this so I can help you." This frustrates him. It doesn't make sense. That's what he wants to know, too. He wants to know so he can tell you. Nor does he need to have someone say, "This is the way, step by step, because this is the way I went." He doesn't need that either. He must find the way for himself, to a degree, at least. Guidelines should have already been set down for him before he reached this age. Now it is rather, "I'm here and I am ready to help you, son."

Then a third principle is that teen-agers need wholesome opportunities to express independence. This is what Dr. Grace Overton, a specialist in this field, calls his "separateness." We really don't "untie" the apron strings during adolescence; we ought to be "loosening" them over a long period of time. Gradually the day comes when the ties are removed. Then he's ready to meet the world. It's when these apron strings have been tied too tightly and we want to cut them with a knife (or he cuts them with a knife) that we have troubles. Rather, it's gradually enabling him to go through experiences and gain some confidence of his own. The teen-ager will then be making some decisions of his own. Actually what we do to help him in this experience is to set up (in every area of his life) acceptable ranges. Within these acceptable ranges (as he matures and moves into adulthood) we allow him more freedom and decision-making. Now, if it's a range, there's a borderline. There is a stopping place.

Take his finances, for example. He has now reached the place where he has his own allowance — his own budget. You have said from the very beginning, "Now these are things you can spend it for; these are not." Within this range he can now make his own decisions about how he'll spend this money. Many times he will choose unwisely, but still within the range. It will be Christian; it will be moral, honest, and ethical; but it may not be the best. He won't always choose the best. But when he steps out of that range and uses some of that money to buy the wrong thing, he has stepped out of the Christian, moral, ethical range. Then you say, "Son, we thought you were mature enough now, but your childhood is showing. You have reverted back." So you deal with him as a child and discipline him as a child.

Guiding your daughter, you say, "Now we are coming to the place where you can buy your clothes." If you have reared this girl well, you have already set up the range with reference to modesty. Sometimes she'll come home with some unusual things: all the girls are wearing them!! But, at least they are modest. The day she buys something that is immodest, she has stepped over the borderline. Then you must be firm.

As young people leave childhood and mature, this range will gradually broaden. The apron strings will be loosened even more. And when we do it this way, they will develop in a healthy way — emotionally, morally, and spiritually. And they will gradually learn to handle their situations better. They will have some help in finding their way. This will give them increased separateness.

There are many things which to teen-agers are symbolic of separateness. For example, a separate room is important. If there is ever a time when a family ought to make a financial sacrifice for a youngster to have a separate room, it is during adolescence. This is a good investment. It's an important one. And there are some other things which give him increased understanding of his maturity. He learns by doing. He'll do and choose the wrong things, but he'll learn from them. It's a sort of trial and error system. Here he'll be very childlike, and there he'll show real maturity. Seeking separateness has its ups and downs, but it builds healthy personality.

The fourth suggestion is that most of the major decisions of life are made during the teens. The young person will probably make a religious decision during this period. Then his selection of life's companion and God's will in reference to life's work will be considered during adolescence. So we have a real stewardship in helping him in decision-making.

(1) As teen-agers mature spiritually, we must guide them in applying the theory of their experience to real living. It's what Gordon Allport[2] said was the shift from saving faith to the maturing faith. The child has the saving faith in his childhood experience at eleven or twelve — he felt it in his heart; but it is put to the test in junior and senior high school, and starting life's work and a family. Therefore, we guide him to put to work, to put into practice, this new Christian life.

(2) We need to guide him in reference to the selection of his life's companion. Aren't you thankful that we can be parents of young people in our Western culture? Our youngsters can select and find the person in God's will as a life companion. They have the freedom to make friends. Aren't you glad that some marriage broker doesn't call you on the phone one day and say, "Mr. Smith has employed me to enter into negotiations with you with reference to the possible marriage of their son to your daughter. The first thing we'll have to know is how much dowry you have saved to pay the family if the boy will marry your girl"? This is still going on in our world.

Suppose you were a parent in a country today where the marriages are not arranged through brokers but through families for various reasons of finance or prestige. When your son or daughter walked down the aisle for marriage, he would have never seen his new life partner. How wonderful it is for our youngsters to have the opportunity of choice in the environment of school, community, and church. They have the opportunities of an ingroup in the church

[2] Gordon W. Allport, *The Individual and His Religion* (New York: The Macmillan Co., 1950).

where they can meet the right kind of young people. This ingroup — the Christian group — is a place where at least some of the things they imitate will be better things.

(3) And then we can guide them regarding life's vocation. One can't think of any time in the history of our race when young people have had more opportunities to find a way of life. They can find a vocation that will be personally satisfying to them and adjusted to their own aptitudes and interest. The freedom with which they can select and the possibilities are unlimited. It's fascinating to study a vocational index and see the various means of livelihood. And all of this gives us a wonderful opportunity to show them new ways in which they can live their lives in Christian stewardship.

The Christian family can build a readiness and expectancy which is most significant. The young person develops a "set" to wholesome vocational attitudes. He looks forward to a life of fulfillment and service, vocationally. In the context of the Christian home, his basic faith, his attitude toward marriage, and his vocational readiness can all form a solid foundation for living.

Thus, in summary, we understand that adolescence is a natural period of development in which young people seek to find their way; express their separateness; and make major life decisions. With this background, the parent begins to understand how the teen-ager matures and grows up emotionally.

GROWING UP EMOTIONALLY THROUGH CONVERSATION

Mary Smith came home from the girls' club crying. Her mother and father stood astounded for she had highly anticipated the meeting. Why was she this way?

Parents of young people understand this type of behavior on the part of adolescents. Young people are *sensitive to failure*. As they are developing emotional balance, the wise leader does not necessarily protect her girls from failure. She is helpful and understanding of their emotional release when they have not succeeded.

Also youngsters are growing up emotionally with the characteristic *mixture of emotions.* They are trying to define their real feelings — with difficulty. It is interesting to see how young people will express both love and hate in a single activity. They will rapidly shift back and forth between loyalty and rebellion or the establishment of the new. Such emotion may even relate to family or the church.

This shifting back and forth is merely the youngster's attempt to get on an even keel emotionally.

Therefore, this means that *emotional loyalties must be harnessed by the church and the Christian home.* They can be channeled to Christ, His church, and the home.

There must be also *a balance of emotional expression and intellectual decision.* As the young person is seeking his emotional balance, he will also shift between emotion and reasoning. You observe this at a religious service where there is a strong appeal. Such shifting is actually a good characteristic, since true religious experiences always have both emotional and intellectual content. One can help by guiding the young person to find a good balance between these two.

Finally, young people are emotionally attached to their peer group. These can be happy emotional attachments, and healthy ones, if properly guided.

During the early teens there is rapid *factual learning.* In fact, they are taking in and seeking to use material with such fluency, that they often appear to be "smart aleck." This is due chiefly to the things they learn in conversation. The youngster is actually astounded at himself with the amount of knowledge taken in.

A few years ago I got into conversation with a thirteen-year-old girl. Before long, to my astonishment, I found out that she was interested in archaeology. As I talked I became surprised at her profound understanding of the field. In attempting to see how far she had gone, I brought up some technical points about the field of Egyptology and Assyriology. To my amazement she had a rather good technical knowledge of these two fields.

One is reimpressed with the fact that young people today are well informed. It means then that our leadership must be particularly stimulating to them!

They are coming into what we call *"judgmentive"* learning. This means that the youngster can make good and wise decisions. Many of them have already made good spiritual decisions. Before long they will be making marriage and vocational choices. They need guidance and understanding.

Also their learning evidences their curiosity. The parent is aware of the fact that this can lead into danger zones as well as being an advantage. This natural, God-given curiosity must be used by the teen-ager to find new healthy experiences and to accumulate good knowledge. But as with most of the gifts in life, it can be misused.

Another aspect of their learning is *creative thinking*. This is actually a combination of judgmentive, decisive, and curiosity thought patterns. That is, he has taken in the factual material but now he is able to create new ideas in his thinking. This can be well directed, if a parent is wise enough to constantly supply a youth with new and exciting experiences.

GROWING UP EMOTIONALLY THROUGH READING

Behavior today certainly verifies the psychologists' principle that young people are highly imitative and suggestible. If one watches television programs produced for adolescents, he is convinced of the fact that young people copy their lives from the examples of others much more than we realize. Thus the power of imitation and suggestion is very strong.

One way in which this influence confronts young people

is through the printed page, television, and radio. Good literature, which emphasizes real people in real-life situations with justifiable rewards and punishments for their acts, has constructive influences. Poor literature, in which justice is missing, exerts destructive influences. There is such a high level of identification and transference in the reading process that our homes have a wonderful opportunity as we suggest and prescribe reading to our young people.

Great literature usually finds its subject matter in the lives of human beings as they face life's crises. The way in which they adjust to real life situations and the solutions they find to these problems constitute strong and suggestible teaching for readers. Someone has said that all of the world's problems can be reduced to man's problems. Thus, all great literature will probably center around man's problems. From the early biblical history of man's temptation by evil, and his subsequent adjustments to that temptation, to the modern novel involving man's relationship to God, Satan, and his fellowman, there lies a great body of helpful literature. The inclusion of materials with high biblical content, then, is strategic to the home library. There is a large constituency of young readers for whom biblical application to everyday conduct is acceptable. However, other teen-agers have difficulty in understanding Scripture. Therefore, living literature which is not biblical can also serve a purpose. This tells about the lives of human beings adjusting to life today. Young readers ought to have contact with both.

Living literature can serve as warning. The example of another's life, found in a book, can often serve as warning to the reader. A good example of this is the young person reading biographical material about the life of someone who has succeeded. The mistakes and misconceptions of the biographical subject can often forestall the same mistakes in the life of a young reader. This is simply leading the reader to prepare for the task of living by study. He takes for granted that he will use books in preparing for other functions of life. How sad that he often fails in his preparation for living life itself.

This means that a well-programmed reading schedule can have a "preventive" effect on youth even as we understand preventive medicine.

In addition, a reader of good literature learns that no two people find the same solution for similar problems. This lesson is worth many hours of sacrificial reading for the young person. From the positive side, a well-balanced reading program suggests that there are many avenues to success as well as to the adjustment of problems. Therefore, reading about the life situations of both Biblical and contemporary characters can cause the reader to be forewarned with reference to life situations. Such reading can also enable him to be "forearmed" as he faces the successive encounters with important life issues.

Living literature can be poetic justice. Yesterday's adolescent psychology book deals with the problems of a youngster's dual standards in life. The modern adolescent psychology text now uses the term, "multiple standards." This gives us the idea that there is such a multiple value system confronting every person that confusion is often the result. The writers of yesterday were much concerned with the right scales of values in their writing. Reward for the hero and punishment for the villain was called "poetic justice." Much of today's literature has a confusion of values. As a recent television commentator said, "We will allow literature to come into our homes through television which we would never allow in our homes through literature."

After a pre-review of much contemporary literature, radio, and television, one wonders about the scale of values here. Therefore, in the books it stocks, a home or church library can sharpen up the ethical, spiritual, and moral values set forth. Fiction can often make justice more obvious than even biographical material. However, the Bible presents the best example of good literature with exacting poetic justice.

Living literature is motivation. The late Dr. George W. Truett said, "The reading of good biographical material was, next to the reading of the Scripture, the most motivating to young people." He placed great stock in the beneficial results of good reading. The home that can provide a good selection of literature by and about men's lives will be motivating.

Most of us think we are not privileged to live near people whose lives are inspiring. However, we can read about the lives of these great ones and receive the same motivation. Through the vehicle of such books many young Christians have found the motivation for life. Thus, a constant and repeated reading of this literature motivates and makes life "goalward." The application of the Hebrew tradition, "As a man thinketh in his heart, so is he," is good here.

A leading American psychologist recently suggested that insecure boys read *Robinson Crusoe.* He added that imaginative reading is helpful for the humorless young person. He continued to elaborate by saying: "Light reading is good for the depressed; books about great people for those who need inspiration; imaginative and yet constructive adventures for those whose lives are drab; and books to encourage creative thinking will actually bring forth creative living from readers." Good literature always motivates men.

Living literature can be inspirational. All biblical and much secular literature actually sets standards which are either difficult or almost impossible for the reader to achieve. Unless one understands the true psychology and theology of spiritual standards, this fact will appear to frustrate the young reader. However, he soon learns that he strives toward the Christian life of perfection although he intellectually knows he cannot achieve it.

Secular literature which gives some element of escapism

without leading to real life responsibility can be very harmful, on the other hand. Yet, this "inspiring" literature has given many the vision for doing great things.

Some youth find difficulty in locating ideal goals in the seemingly drab life which appears to surround them. Thus, in the creative reality of written and visual material such inspiration can sometimes be initiated.

Good reading is a skill and habit as well as a personal interest. Therefore, it must be developed, exercised, and fed. This becomes a real ministry for a Christian parent toward his son or daughter.

KNOWING TODAY'S PITFALLS IN THE JOURNEY

"Are our teen-agers tempted by the same sins as young people of past generations?" Do they face the same pitfalls of temptation on their strange journey?

The answer is complex — it is both yes and no. The basic sins are just the same in all generations. A teen-age boy today is tempted by the same sins and weaknesses as young Moses, Joseph, and other Bible youths. Yet, these same sins are clothed in different form today. The devil changes the outward form of these same sins to make them more appealing to a given age.

Many parents have discipline problems with their youngsters now because these fathers and mothers do not realize that the devil has "modernized" the outward forms of sin. What are some of the sutble sins toward which our youngsters are tempted? Most of them will not be tempted daily to kill or steal or gamble, but they will find these following temptations in their paths.

The modern sin of material competition is everywhere. Our grandparents, as children, were familiar with the admonition, "Thou shalt not covet." But parents today are teaching them to "keep up with the Joneses." We live to catch up with others; we drive to gain the same possessions as they.

Since there are always those who have achieved more than we, this way of life becomes most frustrating. Whereas our forefathers were somewhat content with success in a given area or sphere, we never seem to find the end of it all. *Certainly we do not want to become self-satisfied — yet we ought to be happy with our level of success.*

I'm thinking of a young married couple who did not set their own values and ideals for their marriage at the time of its beginning, but chose another couple (we'll call them Smith) as their pattern. They didn't really know that having what the Smiths had would not make them happy. They both worked for three years to accomplish this, not taking time to "count their many blessings" as they went along. They were almost to the Smith's "level" when they noticed that the Joneses had still more material properties. They abandoned the first goal and tried to catch up with the Joneses. On and on this went through the years. They are still not satisfied, not happy!

Parents ought to be very careful not to live before their teen-agers in such ways as to show that they place more value on the material than on the spiritual.

The modern sin of dissatisfaction is growing. Do your young people find themselves dissatisfied with their present age level — that is, are they trying to grow up before their time? So many of them want to be with older people, want to take on the characteristics of those who are much older. A psychologist cautions people of all ages not to attempt to live beyond their maturity level. The tendency begins in school and proceeds through life. It can grow into constant frustration if we let it. *They should say with Paul, "In whatsoever state I am, in that will I be content."*

We might add here that it is also sinful so to worship youth that one does not want to grow old. Many adults spend all of their time and money trying to look and act younger. They are telling the world that they are not satisfied with God's plan of life. I think God wants us to make ourselves as attractive as we can, but not to be so obsessed with the idea as to neglect service to Him. Perhaps parents can prevent these tendencies in growing young people by not exhibiting it in themselves.

The modern sin of worshiping position opens the door to other temptations. Do they blindly accept the popular pattern of being "well-rounded"? Recently a youth group was told that it would be a pleasure to meet a person who dared to be different. The listeners were shocked because young people today have been taught to place social acceptance by all groups and factors as primary in life. It is the fad to achieve in as many fields as possible. People must be members of every organization and participate in everything. If they all continue to strive for this ultimate "well-roundedness," they will all end up alike! Wouldn't life be boring then?

The really happy, productive and creative people of history have followed a personally selected pattern in life. They have not worried about satisfying every influence in society. They have dared to evaluate for themselves what they wanted and placed everything else in a secondary position. They didn't let the blind desire to be accepted by everyone and every group rule their lives.

Lead your teen-agers to follow the only workable plan for happy and meaningful living — Christ's life as the example. If they live according to His pattern, they will be "well-balanced" without over-concern for reputation.[3]

The modern sin of false security is part of our times. Our big question today is, "faith in God or faith in things"? Where are our youth getting their sense of security?

Do they strive for selfish independence and look toward financial security? Are they already worried about "social security"? The past generation has inferred that we can truly

[3] Chester Swor, *If We Dared!* (Nashville: Broadman Press, 1961), pp. 23ff.

become "independent." We have unconsciously thought
that it was attainable. Many of us will wake up some morning late in life and see the futility of our striving. "Man is
basically a dependent creature." We come near a degree of
an *independence* late in childhood, but that is lost in our
conversion experience, when we must fall back upon complete *dependence* on God — just as we were dependent on
our parents at physical birth. Then again in adult life we
work for independence and security and think we're about
to achieve it when time begins to take its toll in physical and
emotional breakdown, and we are thrown back again in
old age.

Don't let your young people suffer from the same mistakes.
Help them to *make up their minds to understand better the
desire* for "independence." They can never really find it in
the world's meaning of the term. Just as man's financial security and independence comes from his *dependence* on
money in a bank, so does their independence come from
dependence on God. Teach your youth, by example, the
value of depending on God for security.

Thus, *let us nurture in our youth a focus on the simple
and really genuine of life. When the later years draw nigh,
they will not be tempted by the old sins of covetousness, am-
bition, envy, and greed.*

For additional reading see: Fayly H. Cothern, *So You Want to Be Popular*
(Grand Rapids: Zondervan Publishing House, 1960), Chapter 6.

5. The Family Together

". . . open forum"

"THE FAMILY TOGETHER" is a phrase which pictures times of family fellowship. It denotes the members of the group communicating. The phrase suggests play, work, worship, learning, talking (even a little gossiping) together. It is the family at work in the main task of family living — nurturing and growing in the context of wholesome sharing. Out of this kind of living, spiritual values emerge as real and vital. "And if it seem evil unto you to serve the Lord, choose you this day whom ye will serve; whether the gods which your fathers served that were on the other side of the flood, or the gods of the Amorites, in whose land ye dwell; but as for me and my house, we will serve the Lord" (Joshua 24:15).

The "together" part of the phrase is of prime significance. What Elton and Pauline Trueblood call the "withering away of the family" can be remedied by the family coming together again. There will not be togetherness unless there is dialogue in the family. Dialogue needs common interests and activities in which all are involved.

The lack of these common family functions constitutes the problem. In a study by Joseph Fletcher[1] he concludes that the typical family has retained (basically) only one of its seven functions. These functions are, he suggests:

(1) *The productive function.* This has left the home and gone to the factory or the office. The home is no longer the place where we produce our goods in an industrial society. When the economic role of the family, a vital one, is reduced to consumption only, this is a serious form of dysfunction.

(2) *The protective function* whereby the home was once a fort or castle is now handed over to police power, and rightly so. Much is taken from the parents' role of provider and protector. Yet its loss is another in a vital series.

(3) *The educative function.* The methods and curriculum of our modern school system are such that parents simply cannot train and instruct their children at home. Think, then, what this means in terms of the parents' loss of stature in the eyes of children, as they early and daily depend upon non-familial resources.

(4) *The recreative function.* As with education, so recreation has been almost separated from the home. The massive technology of entertainment takes it out of the home, puts it in the school's constantly proliferating extra-curricular program, and in commercial or public places. The hearth-game for the gathered family is gone.

(5) *The religious function* of the family, like all the others, has been transferred to another institution, the church. The Christian emphasis on corporate worship in "God's house" instead of in the home, long ago broke piety and religious nurture away from its family setting. In recent years, the churches have been waking up to this, perhaps too late. Their efforts to inculcate faith and ideals in young people are useless without equivalent cultivation in the home. But

[1] Unpublished paper at Southwestern Baptist Theological Seminary, Fort Worth, Texas.

by now, parents leave all "that sort of thing" to Sunday schools and weekly worship, with clergy and religious teachers as "experts" to carry the whole load. Religion has been professionalized.

(6) *The social function is nearly lost.* It has been taken away from the family. No longer is it the *status-giving institution.* This is true in any democratic society. One's place in the world, his role expectation and social status, are no longer a matter of who he is by birth. It is what we personally achieve, more than by what our "family background" happens to be that counts.

(7) *The affectional function,* the intimate business of love-making, procreation, and child care, is the family's only remaining business. Whether and for how long this function, the only survivor of the seven historic functions remain, is the question.

Therefore, the family must function together in many areas so that there is enough common interest to stimulate conversation. The true family functions were related to survival, interdependency, and spiritual things. Therefore, their very vitality caused conversation about the "really important things." Reuel Howe says that we spend too much family time discussing the unimportant.

A return to true family life with its needed functions will call for involvement in several areas. These may not be the "original ones," but are the ones to which we could return in our contemporary day — they are workable in our times. The successful "rediscovery" of them will not be easy, but it is possible.

To a great extent, their rediscovery is dependent upon the repositionizing of the child in the family as already discussed. In addition, the father and mother roles must be re-evaluated. This we shall do next. Then discussions will follow on these needed functions — which all relate to the family together. They will be (1) the family learning together, (2) the family playing together, (3) the family vacation and recreation, (4) the family in worship and prayer.

RE-EVALUATING PARENTAL ROLES

Neurotic tendencies on the part of the parents highly dispose toward possible neuroses in children. Even friction and bickering by parents has an affect on a child. The ways in which fathers and mothers live out their positions are highly significant.

We are just beginning to understand how impressionable a child really is — even an infant. Jersild tells of experiments where recordings of classical languages were played by the cribs of a conditioned group of babies. Later, when they were in their early teens, these youngsters, and an uncontrolled group, were taught several languages. In almost every case the controlled group could learn those same classical languages with more facility.

Therefore, parental action and stance are worthy of evaluation. This is particularly true of the father-mother roles. Parental domination, over-protection, or over-permissiveness all take their toll in the adjustments of the child. Habits, thoughts, and disposition of a child are largely formed by the attitudes and actions of parents.

Parents today are having difficulty establishing proper father and mother roles. This was discussed briefly in chapter 3 in the material on the changing family pattern. Additional attention here is warranted as we look at the whole family together.

The father's place in the Hebrew home was one of temporal and spiritual leadership. This was, of course, true in most families of the past. We take it for granted that today's father is less the authority and leader. This may not be altogether true.

Elizabeth Hurlock cites a study which indicates that children still see their father as superior and senior in the family.

He is also pictured as one who punishes the hardest, owns more, knows more, and is the "head of the house." This may be stereotyped or generalized, yet one usually cannot fool children!

The position of the father in many earlier cultures was less clearly the "provider" role than in some contemporary cultures. Farming, hunting and home provision were often the wife-mother tasks. Even in more recent civilizations (where the father worked at home on a farm or in a shop connected with the house) his providing role was shared with his wife. The industrial revolution did much to bring about "division of labor" in homes as well as in business and industry. Father "went to work." This estrangement of father working away from home while mother stayed at home had psychological and social reactions. It caused some children to feel more distant from the father. The withheld discipline (often postponed until the father's return) added to the estrangement. This has been overcome more recently because modern fathers play with their children more than their forefathers did. Affection and comradeship between a father and his children should develop early. This bridges the estrangement gap.

In the ancient family (particularly Hebrew or Oriental) the father was also priest and judge. He settled spiritual and family (or clan) problems. His role as spiritual leader and teacher was never questioned. Even today the eldest male in a Jewish home has priestly duties during the religious holidays.

Fathers in our culture share more parental responsibility with their wives. If they lead in family worship and give real security to the home, they can hold the "father" position and yet not be dictators. In seeking to nurture the democratic processes in a family, neither parent should sacrifice his leadership position. It is a partnership, but with each parent retaining his "father" and her "mother" figure completely.

The father's spiritual role is a most interesting one for the Christian home. All spiritual understandings are based on non-spiritual understanding. We cannot really "think" in the abstract. Therefore, Jesus used the human position of "father" to give man a mental vehicle for thinking "God." In Christ's day the father's position in a family (or tribe) was a good human parallel. Today there is a problem, of course, when something like the following happens.

Mrs. Elizabeth Baker was teaching a group of primary children in her church. She had just referred to God as father when little Evelyn leaned over to another primary girl and whispered, "If he's like my daddy, I'm not so sure I'd like to live with him in heaven at all!"

Unless fathers exemplify the true father's characteristics such comparisons are meaningless or even harmful.

God is Father — in fact, He created fatherhood. From Adam down to the contemporary father, God creates. When God wanted to reveal the great mystery of His love, He showed it in His perfect "Son." Thus, God in the person of Jesus, saw Himself as "Father."

The creativity which the heavenly Father gave the fathers of men — made in His spiritual image, leaders of families, procreators of children, and spokesmen for God — all amplify this fatherhood of man.

Thus, it is reasonable that God should command that the fathers of children teach the Lord's testimonies to their children. This priestly role is at home in family living. The subject of family worship led by a father is inseparable from any study of fatherhood.

The father's leadership of family worship is important enough to merit a special word here. Donald F. Ackland says that it is desirable for the man of the house to assume this responsibility. Christian fathers should think of such leader-

ship as a privilege. Spiritual leadership should only fall upon
the mother when the father is not spiritually qualified, he
says.

In reading the remaining portion of this chapter on worship, the reader should bear in mind this responsibility of
the father. Place the father in the leadership role. Then
consider his psychological image, too. Freud said that the
child's concept of God is in every case modeled after the
father. This would include the conscious concept as well
as the child's unconscious view.

The overall behavior of the father will condition, therefore,
his place in family worship. How he schedules his time, his
representation of security and permanency, his contact with
wife and children — all regulate this.

The time he spends with his family helps positionize his
role for worship. If he seems to be too busy to be with his
family, he suggests a heavenly Father who is really not interested in His children.

For an example, I have a friend who has two boys. He is
a busy and successful photographer. His time — day and
night — is worth money. Yet, when his sons were young, he
would regularly place in his engagement book at his studio
these words, "Stay at home and be with the family!" Sometimes the date-book advised: "No appointments this afternoon — play with the boys!" This kind of family living builds
a father's role and image so that he can lead in family worship.

The mother's place in the Hebrew home was one of new-
found honor and prestige. In most of the Oriental cultures
of ancient times, the mother had little respect in the family
circle. She was a servant of the husband and custodian of
the family and domestic responsibilities. With the rise of
the Hebrew nation, new prestige became involved. This
had a background with the ancient Hebrews. In Genesis
17:16 the verse reads, "Yea, I will bless her and she shall

be a mother of nations." A new woman suffrage developed into honor for motherhood among these Hebrew peoples.

Mrs. Edith Deen in her book, *Family Living in the Bible* (Harper and Row, New York, 1963), devotes an entire chapter to motherhood in the Bible. She emphasizes the biblical backgrounds to motherhood and particularly the place of the mother in the family circle.

These mothers of yesterday exerted great influence in the family, even though the elder males usually held the higher official positions. The mother's teaching of the children and handling of domestic affairs indirectly caused her to have unofficial honor. Many great biblical characters learned the scriptures and the testimonies of the Law from their mothers as well as fathers. Mrs. Deen points out that in any number of scriptures the terms "father" and "mother" are listed as equals. In one instance the mother is even mentioned before the father. This does not seem so significant in our day, but when it is noted in the context of the Oriental world it is most unusual.

These women who were the teachers and heads of their houses were capable women. A job description of their responsibilities would probably not be as varied as that of a contemporary mother but would certainly show diversity. These women were truly "queens of their castles." When you consider some of the difficult and oppressive conditions under which they lived, their leadership in the home is even more remarkable.

Mothers in our own culture played a significant role in the establishment of the United States. The pioneer mothers of the Eastern seaboard reared men who were capable of the ideas involved in the Bill of Rights and the Declaration of Independence. Their daughters were the women who led husbands and sons into the great Western plains and established the Western Empire. The pioneer mother in Ponca City, Oklahoma, is portrayed in bronze holding the hand of her son, with her Bible under her other arm. These were strong, moral women who were really "the mothers of a nation."

Their pride was in their families and homes and it was from this first unit that the states grew. Finally the states became the great commonwealth of states and then a nation. Any nation which loses the honorable role of motherhood begins to deteriorate at the basic unit of its construction — the family.

This is the fallacy of a communistic system. There are no family units with strong parental guidance to provide the first unit of government. This unit is essential.

The mothers of yesterday worked through the team of the family — with every member having its own chores. This provided a common sharing in family living that was edifying and character building. The mother was usually the foreman of this team and the real hub of the wheel of cooperation and sharing. The dominance of the father in family life (frequently brought over from Europe) soon died away. The father and mother functions soon became cooperating roles. The family was led through a partnership bound together by Christian and romantic love. Out of this beginning the modern democratic family processes evolved and children were reared in what Frances Tyler calls "the little world of home."

However, it is conceivable that the parental role has become so liberalized in our day that both father and mother have lost their leadership positions. As stated earlier, the mother in the American home needs to re-establish her position as queen of the palace of the home and mother of her children in the fullest sense.

The mother of today is a sophisticated person with considerably more technical help in managing her household and rearing her children. The irony is, however, that this learning has not always produced a better home or a better family. Yet, we must not discount the many thousands of capable young women who in honesty and dedication give themselves to their family responsibilities. They utilize the new findings of psychology and sociology and actually carry out a splendid job of motherhood.

These mothers are the best informed in history. They have more resources at their fingertips to do a superb job of family living. These sophisticated and independent women are the true teachers of today. When they cease to function fully in their didactic role and turn all such responsibilities over to school (and even the church) they have lost their significance. Many of these women today are going to have to decide between the preeminence of the mother role or the many calls from community and social life. The re-establishment of the mother role can only come when individual women recommit themselves to its responsibilities.

These women need to use all the resources at hand without making motherhood a scientific business. The emotional and spiritual love and affection, which have always been necessary, are still needed. The mother-child relationship must be one of intimacy and personal contact. Her teaching methods will be informal and subtle and will be in a climate entirely different from public school or other educational institutions. However, this kind of teaching can be the most effective in the history of the human race. She must take motherhood as a serious business, a living business, a loving business.

The mother of tomorrow may have a more difficult time than the mother of today. As the image and model of the mother in the home continues to disintegrate, conscientious women will find it more difficult to function in this role. The hand that used to rock the cradle now operates the I.B.M. machine, opens the bank vault, raises the gavel in the meeting, sits on the elected board of the church, and receives the gubernatorial appointments of her state. These capable yet fragmented women will find it increasingly hard to regain a family role in the years to come. Yet, if conscientious women will consider marriage and motherhood as a spiritual call *directed by God's will* they can take their present resources and advantages available and do a better job in the home than has ever been done before. From a human standpoint, there can be no greater hope for the race than that of Christian motherhood.

The Family Learning Together

Man is created in God's image, but he is placed on earth in an immature state — infancy. With the help of God, and persons around him, the infant develops gradually. It takes years of learning for him to become mature. In fact, the learning process never ceases. Adults of mature years are still learning new ways to live and adjust to life's experiences. The *family* was not established merely for propagation; *its full purpose also includes teaching*.

As the young person matures, he gradually separates himself from the family. He learns more from influences outside the family as this separation takes place. He is shifting from dependence in the family to independence. As long as he is growing up in the house of his parents, however, the home is his most effective school. A successful separation from the home may come when he is older, if the teaching has been good.

The home, ordained by God and perfected under Christ, is an *ideal teaching institution*. Two people devoted in Christian and romantic love, can build a home that is an excellent teaching agency.

In the early years of marriage a couple spends much time learning from each other. We call this kind of learning adjustment. It is prerequisite to the necessary give-and-take of matrimony. Just as atmosphere is so important to learning in a school, home atmosphere is significant. The environment of the Christian home provides the needed support for a couple during this period. Then, they become teachers when children come into the family circle. Young parents immediately begin a teaching process as they guide the children in learning skills for living.

Every room in the house becomes a classroom. In the kitchen the child learns to feed himself and understand his physical needs for food. In the bathroom he is taught the virtues of cleanliness. In the living room he is taught the social graces, and there he learns how to meet strangers and behave according to our cultural standards. In the dining room the child is taught manners which will become a part of his personality. He also learns, in the dining room, the custom and reality of expressing appreciation to God at the table. He sees family solidarity as the members gather around the table to pray, eat, and enjoy fellowship.

The child sees the value and dignity of honest work as he watches his father work in the garage, basement, or workroom. Later, he begins to engage in work himself. Thus he learns to use his hands and mind. Truly, every room in the house is a classroom for learning.

The home, as the child's first school, largely determines his success in other relationships, such as the church and school. *The child learns by doing* and watching as well as from formal teaching. These methods of teaching also are used in our modern schools.

For example, our grandmothers studied "natural science" by means of a lecture and an illustrated textbook. In the book was a picture and a diagram of a dissected frog. Teenagers today hear a lecture on the physical makeup of a frog. Then they go into the biology laboratory and study a real frog. Finally, these students dissect and analyze the actual object in the laboratory.

LEARNING BY EXAMPLE

Even as we learn so much by the laboratory method of doing things, *we also learn from the example* of the acts and lives of others. It is a well-known principle of education that we learn more by example than from statistics and facts. In the family we are constantly teaching one another by the example of the lives we live. We weaken our opportunities when we teach one thing and live another. The young mother and father, for example, can teach the child honesty by using the Bible and setting up certain rules in the home. This procedure ought to be followed; but it will lose its effectiveness if children see the parents failing in any way to practice these principles of honesty.

Wise parents arrange experiences and activities in family life which teach each family member the same principles they try to teach verbally. Think back to the teachers you had in elementary school. Do you remember the subject matter they taught you, or do you remember them as persons? Probably as persons first. Ideally, you would remember what they taught you and their personalities too!

It has always been obvious that the teacher-parent is important in the whole teaching process. The example set by the life of the parent is as important as the things taught by the parent. Learning is a broad process indeed.

When a teacher ceases to learn from his pupils, he stops being a good teacher. When a parent cannot learn from his child, he is missing some of the best opportunities of parenthood.

What are some ways in which parents may learn from their children? Parents can learn *by listening*. When parents let children talk, they find out the children's ideas, their misconceptions, and their new-found interests. When parents regularly prohibit children's comments, they limit one of the best methods of understanding children.

Parents, who are teachers, learn from sons and daughters

by playing with them. The natural, free expressions encouraged in play are most revealing. Parents can learn more about the children's problems if they will play with them.

Parents can learn problem-solving *by watching a child* solve a simple problem. This is an inspiration to a parent who has been struggling with his own problems. Adults can learn from the young that many difficulties can be handled in simple fashion.

Parents can learn the simple faith of the child. Jesus gathered the children around Him and used them as perfect examples of the kind of faith His followers ought to have.

Husbands and wives also learn from each other. When they do things together, they constantly influence (teach) each other. Clever wives may arrange experiences which lead their husbands to accept their ideals. This indirect type of teaching utilizes the laboratory method. Jesus led His disciples to "do" certain things, and they learned from these activities as much, no doubt, as they learned from the Saviour's more formal teachings. In addition, when they accepted the things which they had seen in Christ's life and their own experience, they retained those lessons better.

Thus, when people miss normal family life, they do not have the advantages of the home as a school. In family living we learn skills for the rest of life.

We learn from each other. For the child, the home is a school in which he learns to cooperate, share, obey, and even sacrifice. He learns from his teachers who are also his parents. He learns some things by their teaching, others by imitating them. Thus, their lives as parents and Christians ought to be acceptable.

Adults also learn through experience in the home. Parents profit from their association with the children. Wives and husbands learn from each other. These families must be together enough to regain the family functions of learning together!

THE FAMILY PLAYING TOGETHER

Although, of necessity, families will face many problems, family life ought to be happy. Ideally, one ought to be anxious to get home to his family. Mother and children should enjoy one another all day and anticipate the arrival of husband and father. In short, family living should afford some of the most joyous times in all of life. Nothing in this life is more admirable than a happy, wholesome, Christian family at play together.

Healthy people need to have fellowship with people of their own ages. Our churches, schools, and fine civic organizations provide this "graded" recreation. However, none of this will substitute for the happy relationships within the family circle. The give and take of family play and recreation is essential. It also develops a sense of humor between members of the family group. This may prove vital at some later time of family difficulty. We are going to look at the play within the family and with friends visiting in the home. In this fellowship in the home families will be able to apply Christian principles.

Play and recreation have become commercialized. We need a revival of participation type activities in the home. We've forgotten how much fun we find in making candy together; in making a family game out of painting the house. Too often we feel we must leave our house to have a good time.

An encouraging trend is the increase of outside cooking by families. The use of the barbecue and outdoor living in the yard or on the patio are wholesome tendencies. The family picnic is coming into its own again.

Another area of enjoyable family activity is entertaining. We do not have family friends in our home as much as our grandparents did. Such contacts with Christian friends, entertained in our homes, are most satisfying. Also they help center interest and attention within the home.

The home must be more than a place to eat and sleep if it is to fulfill its true mission. We must gather, with our friends, in our homes so as to build up a warmth and security within them. Friendships developed in our "houses" change them into "homes."

Also, our friends understand us better when they have been in our homes often, because one's home is typical of his interests and ideals. How many people have you failed to understand and really appreciate until you visited in their homes?

Furniture, dishes, silver, and linens become more valuable when they have been used by friends. Thus entertaining friends in our homes is one of the best forms of family fellowship.

Playing with church friends helps the family. A family which was active in the church found its friendships outside the church. They attended services, served on committees, and participated in programs. Yet they never engaged in the social life of the church. Other families with whom they had fellowship were all non-church people. They came to their pastor stating that they were unhappy, but did not know why. They soon found, with the minister's help, that the inconsistencies in their church life and social life caused their trouble.

One function of a church is to provide wholesome fellowship and social life between church members. Christian families will find happiness in associations which lead them into better spiritual life rather than away from it. In a sense, a church is a large family made up of smaller families where play, recreation, and social contacts are available.

These and many other activities and contacts enhance family play. We might conclude so far that the following values result.

(1) Psychological — When the members of a family play together, a spirit of oneness is fostered. They learn better to

appreciate each other's weaknesses. Loyalties are enhanced, and the members see themselves more as a part of a team. Also, most family play gives each member his opportunity to lead and then, in turn, to follow. Morale grows with family fellowship.

(2) Educational—As we have already discussed, the family members learn from each other. The specialized learning in play is difficult to replace. It is free and informal learning which is most satisfying.

(3) Social — The intimate friendship needed to make family living worthwhile is helped by play and recreation. When a father watches his young son lead in a project, his admiration and fatherly love are projected into the future, and he dreams of the leadership of his son in maturity.

A girl appreciates her mother more when she sees her mother participating in family fun. She likes to see her mother be a girl, too. The social values of family play are almost impossible to estimate. The social bond may be strong enough to help hold the family together in time of strife.

(4) Physical — Recreation and social contacts are needed for healthy living — individually and in the family. Jesus enjoyed family fellowship and social life. How can Christians testify to others that their lives are happy if they are not happy in their own families? Christian fellowship must begin at home.

The Family Vacation

The family vacation is one of the joys of the American family. It offers a time together which encourages more intimate communication than most other occasions.

The "annual" vacation is a high-light in the yearly calendar of thousands of families. The tragedy is, however, that for many this annual vacation is a "fling" of reckless living. A vacation is defined by Webster as, "Respite or time of respites; an intermission of rest. A period for rest and recreation; a holiday."

The trend is to make a "Roman holiday" out of it — this is harmful. Also there is the tendency to attempt to do so much and travel so far that the family returns home tired, tense, and dissipated. There is value in going away from home, but it is, perhaps, unwise to spend all of one's allotted time traveling. This period should provide wholesome relaxation, variety, spiritual and mental refreshing, and interest. Some general suggestions are:

(1) Plan the family vacation well in advance of the time with the entire family participating in some fashion in the plans. Build up a happy anticipation.

(2) Select a theme for the vacation. If it involves traveling to new places, study schools, churches, historic sites, or some other subject matter. This ought to be done in a voluntary, relaxed manner. If it is to a fishing camp, lead the whole family to become interested in fishing. Sometimes a member of the family would rather have an individual interest — this would be fine.

(3) Take advantage of the rest, beauty, and fellowship of the vacation for family prayer and spiritual refreshing. This is particularly enjoyable when the family worship can take place out of doors where one feels close to his Creator.

People who never play are certain to become sick. Recreation and social contacts are needed for healthy living — individually or in the family. How can Christians testify to others that their life is a happy one, if they are not happy in their own families? Christian fellowship must begin there.

Then, the family will want to carry its regular Bible to use in devotion periods. Times of family worship ought not be omitted on the vacation. Prayer should be offered at strange tables, because the same merciful God provides — no matter where we are in His world.

Bible study as well as devotion should be carried on. Parents must see to it that the spiritual part of life "goes on as usual" on the vacation trip.

Third, as suggested earlier, the theme of a vacation trip can be centered around church buildings seen in new places. Another possibility is to study beauties of nature and tie them into Bible verses or passages. For example, if someone sees a swallow on the trip the family might try to remember a verse of Scripture about that bird. When the father sees a herd of cattle on the hillside, he might ask the children if the Bible refers to cattle on the hills.

The thing to emphasize is that God's Word should go with the family wherever it goes — even on the annual vacation!

Whenever possible the family should plan brief vacation periods together. Even a day's retreat will give opportunity for fellowship and conversation in the family. The need for times of relaxation is imperative, if the family would revive its basic functions.

The Family in Worship and Prayer

Nothing unites a family as does praying together. This spiritual unity enables the family to face the difficult issues of life which are certain to come. Prayer places the home in constant contact with God to such an extent that He is not just a guest in the home but is always present in fellowship.

In this discussion consideration will be given to the Bible and its use in family prayer, the place of prayer, the time of prayer, and the values of prayer to the family.

One of the greatest treasures of many families is their family Bible. In many of these Bibles are historical and priceless records of births, marriages, and deaths in that family for generations. As the Bible is passed from parents to children, there is evidence of real unity within the family.

The possession of a family Bible means much in a Christian home, for the Bible and the home are inseparable.

The place for family prayer is very important. Do present-day American homes present the permanency and security of Jewish homes in the past? Many cultural changes have taken place. When our forefathers came to this country, they established homes much like those in Europe. That is, large houses were built to serve two or three generations. In their spacious dining rooms and kitchens the family Bible (often brought from abroad) was read, and family prayer was a part of family living. In recent generations we have been building smaller houses, and each generation lives unto itself. The family has tended to drift apart in its work and interests.

Today the tendency to change houses and furniture frequently prevents children from building a sense of security and stability. Added to this is the trend toward packing away the old family Bible.

The time of family prayer must be considered too. In addition to the problem of a place, we face the problem of a time for family prayer. Each family has its own schedule; therefore, no specific time for prayer can be suggested for all families. The ideal would be, of course, for every family to eat all three meals together and tie in Bible usage and prayer with these three regular gatherings. Many homes are fortunate to be able to do this. Others have a problem in this because of adults working on different shifts and schedules. Sometimes adult work schedules do not coincide with the children's school hours. Such difficulties often necessitate some members' missing the meal with the family. The remaining members should still pray together.

Some families are all together before retiring at night. This hour provides an excellent time for prayer. Also the Sunday dinner meal can become a prayer high-light of the whole week. Just as the Wednesday evening prayer service can be the "hour of power" for a church, the noon meal on Sunday can serve this purpose for the family.

Another time for family prayer is at the time of crisis. When a family faces some difficulty it is usually drawn closer together. Also the spiritual life is enriched when members of the family, often two or three generations, gather together around the Thanksgiving or Christmas dinner table for prayer. Anything parents can do to relate prayer, the Bible, and the home will help.

One of the sweetest hours of prayer is the time spent with a young child just before he goes to bed at night. This experience is enriching for both children and parents. It particularly teaches the child about God's protective powers and the parents' concern for the child's welfare.

In past years the activity of the home centered around the Bible and prayer. The activity of today's home often seems to center around the telephone or the television set. Thus we have broken down the traditional associations of Bible and home, family life and prayer, and "worship at the table."

God is love, and His Word is the Book of love. When the Bible is in the center of the family, there is a stronger bond of love between the members. Most individuals need a spiritual tie to enhance love. People are united when they focus their attention on a single focal point. Church members are knit together by the worship of one God in a service. In the same manner, a family will feel closer to each other at the family worship.

In family worship, love between man and God sets the pattern for love within the family circle. For example, Christ's love must be returned because He first loved us. So must love among members of a family be returned.

According to the pattern of man's love for God, the family learns that love cannot be forced. Even as God will not force us to love Him, so must our love for one another be freely given.

As we come together to worship, we find that our love

must be expressed to God daily. Thus we learn to express our love to one another regularly and freely.

In our devotional life we learn that love for God must be personal. We also love each one in the family circle in a personal way on the basis of that one's own worth. Reading God's Word of love will surely increase our love.

Many times sacrifices must be made as each family works out arrangements for the place and time of family prayer. But values and satisfactions are more than worthy of necessary sacrifices. When the family gathers itself together to express love to God, the pattern is set for better relationships between the members of the group. The children's love for their mother and father is enriched because they have learned to love God at the family time of devotion and prayer.

Family worship is the high moment of the day in the Adams home. Each member of the family, from the pre-school child to the grandmother, looks forward to this daily experience. Each one enters heartily into the worship period, and when it is over each feels in his own way that he, along with the other members of the family, has been close to God.

The Whites live in the same neighborhood and attend the same church. They, too, have family worship regularly. They feel that it is something all church families should do. But for them it is a chore. The Bible and other worship materials never can be found when they are needed. There seems to be no time when all the family are together. There is frequent quarreling over who will lead the discussion, and the smaller children are usually asleep long before it is over.

Many families do not fully understand what family worship can do for the home. Because they do not understand its full potentialities as a spiritual experience, they do not expect enough results or the right kind of results. A family like the Whites can go through the form of worship in the home and gain little from the experience. Another family can enter into family worship more deeply, and the whole spiritual tone of their home will be lifted.

What are some results of meaningful family worship? Here are some benefits which can be expected when families understand the purpose of worship in the home:

Each member of the family actively participates; no one is a passive onlooker.

Certain "high church" groups emphasize a passive service in which the worshiper simply observes a ritual which is overly symbolic. Most evangelical groups, however, believe in active participation in worship. Participation enriches life, teaches and educates, and gives a feeling of belonging. A passive worship experience cannot produce these results.

The same principles apply to family worship. When a family simply listens to a reading and repeats a memorized prayer, the experience may have little more than a certain inspirational value. But the family profits richly from the worship experience in which there is full and active participation by all — when everyone is personally engaged in prayer, when the Scripture passage is examined carefully and time is given to thoughtful comment.

A Christian family can expect family worship to be more valuable to each person as he naturally and actively engages in the experience.

Family worship can and does help meet real life needs.

Although there is spiritual inspiration in family worship, it is also a teaching and learning experience. The message of the Scripture passage and the gratitude and seeking expressed in the prayers is not related in a general way to all things, but is pointed specifically to the life needs of individual members of the family.

Someone has said that next to personal prayer, family prayers should be the most intimate. In the reading of God's Word in the family there also should be a certain warmth and intimacy.

For example, a father may say after having read a verse, "John, do you see any way this may help you in the problem you are now facing in school?" Or a daughter might comment, "Mother, what does that passage have to do with the way I'm supposed to live before my friends?" Such discussions become a kind of laboratory experience in worship.

Perhaps 50% of the content of a good sermon, say some authorities, is teaching. Even preaching, it is seen, is educational as well as inspirational. Thus it is with family worship when God's Word is related to the real problems and needs of everyday life. Then participation is easy because needs are met. People are interested in that which meets their life needs.

One of the miracles of God's Word is its timeliness. It meets the needs of every individual in every way.

Parents must always try to interpret God's Word to children in simple terms. When Jesus explained the Scriptures, His explanations were simple and always related to some vital issue of living. Family worship relates to real life needs as it involves questions, answers, and discussions.

Family worship changes lives.

When members of the family actively engage in worship related to their needs, the experience changes their lives. One cannot go through such a daily experience without feeling its effects. One cannot seek out God's will for his life without his life being changed. God's Word cannot be opened to one whose spirit is ready to hear without results taking place. There are many glowing stories of families that began worship in the home and saw their home life made over.

When it comes to changing lives, families can expect maximum results from family worship. God has promised that when His Word is opened and two or more are gathered to find help, His Holy Spirit is present to give that help.

Conversion experience will come in family worship. Major life problems will be solved. Hardened hearts will be softened and calloused attitudes changed as a result of family worship.

Teen-agers will come to family worship from the frivolous world of school and social competition and leave in serious contemplation of what they will do with their lives. Children will come from play to a simple worship experience and leave with a new understanding of how God and His world relate to their lives. They will return to play with a new concept of sharing, cooperation, and fairness.

A father comes to the experience of family worship with a business problem and leaves with a clear understanding of the course of action a Christian businessman should take.

Yes, family worship — if it is what it ought to be — changes lives.

Results can be measured. If all these things be true of family worship — if it provides active participation, relates to real life, changes lives — then it should stand every test. If the worship experience does these things, the results can be seen in the changed atmosphere of the home.

A family ought to be fair in trying to measure the effects of prayer and Bible reading with discussion. If family worship is a genuine learning and inspirational experience, a family should not be afraid to test it. If an objective test indicates that worship in the home is not getting results through enriched lives, then a family should take action. It is time to change methods, to give the experience more spiritual depth.

A dedicated family engaged in worship in the home is a growing, changing family. It is a family in which each member is becoming more Christlike.

The teaching values of family worship are evident when the family is together. For example, little Randy Moore ran into the house crying bitterly. He had just come from play with the other youngsters in the neighborhood. Slamming the kitchen door, he wailed, "Mother, I won't let those kids play with my new rocket launcher."

Here a typical American mother faced a typical problem. How can this kind of situation relate to what a child learns at home about Christian living?

One way to deal with problems like this is to take advantage of the teaching values in family worship. Mrs. Moore lifted her little son to her lap and began discussing his situation with him. She remembered that the family worship Scripture passage of the day before had been about the good Samaritan. And so drawing from their experiences in worship she attempted to show the child that he must share his playthings with his friends. She pointed out that some of his little friends were not able to have some of the nice things he had. This wise mother was connecting the principles of Jesus to the real life experiences of the child in a way he could understand.

Although every family wants to give major emphasis to the inspirational and worship aspects of the family worship experience, they can also draw from it inherent teaching values and give them practical application in daily experiences. In other words, learning is a goal of family worship and can take place just as can spiritual enlightenment and encouragement. Wise parents relate every aspect of prayer and Bible readings to daily experiences. Here are some ways this is done.

Teaching values can best come out of family worship when the family is really united in this experience. Of all the things that take place in family life, prayer together can unify the home more than almost anything else.

It is interesting how human beings, when they focus their attention on one idea as a prayer theme, can be unified as in no other way. When a group of people focus their attention on a common goal, a new closeness of spirit develops. This is stated in the Scripture passage, "Where two or three are gathered together in my name, there am I in the midst of them" (Matthew 18:20). Few things can unify a family better than focusing their attention upon spiritual things. Out of this kind of atmosphere and experiences great values naturally come. The following are a few obvious teaching values.

The members of the family will come to look upon family prayer as a period for guidance in their daily lives.

It will become a time of confession to one another as well as to God.

Various differences among the members of the family will be put on a more equal footing, since at times each will lead in prayer.

The worship atmosphere in the family will naturally lead them to talk about spiritual and moral questions and problems not likely to be talked about under other circumstances.

Ties of family fellowship will grow in an atmosphere of spiritual fellowship. Many times spiritual ties are even stronger than other ties that bind the family.

Many personal problems will likely be voiced and discussed by the family in the period of family worship.

As the family in worship learns to express love to God, they will also learn to better express love within the family.

Family worship time can also be a time for summarizing the activities of the day. The happiness of the day can be looked at afresh in the light of prayer and Bible truth. The planned activities of the remainder of the day and the following day can be discussed and God's leadership can be requested. When it serves this purpose, family worship is like the prayer the pastor prays at the beginning of a Sunday morning worship service. He as shepherd of the flock reviews the experiences of the church family in the past week, and prays God's blessings upon members who are absent or who face difficulties or illness. As the pastor's summary prayer can be a highlight in the light of a good church, a parent's summary prayer can be a highlight in the life of a family.

In an atmosphere of family inventory and "stock-taking," teaching values will naturally emerge. When Scripture passages such as that about the good Samaritan are read, they often can be directly related to daily living experiences. Certainly God wants a family's spiritual experiences with His Word and prayer to be carried over into life and help the family meet real life problems and situations.

The psalmist says: "We will not hide them [God's words] from their children, shewing to the generation to come the praises of the Lord, and his strength, and his wonderful works that he hath done. For he established a testimony in Jacob, and appointed a law in Israel, which he commanded our fathers, that they should make them known to their children: that the generation to come might know them, even the children which should be born; who should arise and declare to their children" (Psalm 78:4-6).

In this and other Scripture passages is the definite admonition to parents to use the Bible in family life. In this and other passages the teaching aspect and value of God's Word is definitely indicated. Scripture passages can be discussed at home and an application of them can be made to daily family living just as there is discussion and application in Sunday school Bible study. Such discussion includes the often immature questions of young children as well as parental discussions about major family problems and decisions.

There is also a kind of inferred teaching value in the use of the Bible in the home. The use of the Bible strengthens the feelings of security and stability of the whole family. This is more than just the idea that information and inspiration come out of Bible reading. The psychological fact that the Bible *is* read in the home, and recognized as God's Word to the family, gives a sense of stability to the members.

As we think again of Randy Moore coming in from play

with his problem of sharing with neighborhood children, we see that God has intended for the home to be a real life laboratory of learning. Every parent can be a better parent and a better teacher of Christian values by knowing what his child is being taught in Sunday school. Church teaching can be coupled with Bible reading in the home and with the subject of the current prayer life of the family. The home can be a laboratory where spiritual principles are put to work.

The truth brought forth from God's Word should be applied first in the relationships of the family. When these principles are applied there, they will more likely be used by the family members in other community and world relationships. If the members of the Christian family cannot apply spiritual laws within the home, they will have difficulty doing so beyond the home. Only when there is close harmony between what is learned in family worship and what is done in daily living will family worship have its greatest teaching value. For good teaching to result there must be close harmony between theory and practice.

We have seen that every Christian family can enhance its family worship by drawing from its teaching values as well as inspirational values. Although worship is its chief object, family worship can be the springboard for the teaching and application of good values in all of family life. In families where this fuller concept is understood and applied, family worship is both educational and inspirational. Even as the Wednesday prayer meeting can become the source of inspiration for activity in the church family, so daily family worship can become that source of inspiration for Christian teaching in the home.

The family together in fellowship, in evaluation, in learning, in play, in worship, and in prayer should be a happy family. The great Christian scene is the gathered family around the Bible.

6. The Productive Years

". . . conversation vs. preoccupation"

THE MIDDLE YEARS of adulthood are called by Karl Stolz the "age of accomplishment." They are the productive years in terms of mature life contribution and constructive living.

Dialogue may be minimized because of preoccupation with each marriage partner's business responsibilities, community or church service, or grandchildren. However, in most mature and well-adjusted marriages this period (often the children have left) may provide for some of the deepest and richest conversation. Husband and wife have gone through many life issues together. A new, richer intimacy grows and the "transition" of dialogical contact takes place. By this we mean the gradual change from the chatter of young adulthood to quiet, less verbalized contacts of retirement. In between these two dialogical stages there is the rich, full conversation of the middle-aged adult.

Planning for grandchildren, winding up the mortgage on the house, and arranging for retirement, help to cement the relationship. Whenever we *plan together* we are *drawn together!*

Studies indicate that this age group has more common interests in passive sports (where earlier the common interests were in participation sports), serious, non-fictional reading (where before it was less serious and fictional), and interests in serious cultural endeavors. Too, a revival of spiritual concerns is often present. All of this enhances verbal confrontation.

Individual habit systems tend to become more common to each other. This enables each to better anticipate the other's thoughts and actions. Thus, the illusion that they can now "read each other's minds." This finer sensitivity to the spouse helps conversation and understanding, of course.

Yet, the husband may feel less close to his wife, during this time, since in what Oliver calls "the dangerous forties," he may seek new experiences. And the woman may feel insecure because she has lost her place as a needed mother. She may seek to assume a new central role by earning some income, participating in organizations, or fulfilling social roles.[1]

Other psychological and emotional adjustments to the change of life may cause conversational estrangements or lack of real communion and integrity. However, this usually takes care of itself as these biological adjustments are completed.

Thus, these middle years, in spite of some possible trouble zones, can be full and rewarding. They have also become, in our culture, the years of contemplation of retirement.

Robert Browning wrote:

> Grow old along with me!
> The best is yet to be,
> The last of life, for which the first was made:
> Our times are in His hand
> Who saith, "A whole I planned,
> Youth shows but half; trust God; see all, nor be afraid!

[1] Bernard J. Oliver, Jr., *Marriage and You* (New Haven: College and University Press, 1964), p. 266.

The middle years mark achievement and true maturity. Some of the most enjoyable experiences come then. Success in one's children, vocation, and real church service should be typical. How rich and satisfying, if one is properly oriented and if he fights competitive materialism. Yet, many lose this battle — they avoid realities and God's natural process for man, which is "aging"!

WHAT IS ADULTHOOD — REALLY?

Any definition of adulthood, and particularly the middle years, would be difficult and incomplete. However, as the adult relates himself to the family in conversation and dialogue, there are several general characteristics which can be summarized. There are certain psychological and social definitions of adulthood, as it is expressed in our contemporary culture, which are somewhat definable. The period of adulthood, referred to as the middle years, or productive years, is considered by various scholars to be of varying length. Soares sees it as 40-60 years of age; Stolz as 35-55. Maves agrees with Soares, as does Brewbaker.

(1) *Middle adulthood is a time of leadership and control.* This is an adult-centered world. Even though we have shifted in the emphasis of the age of leadership, by and large, world affairs are led by mature people. The elder statesman still is looked to with respect in national and world affairs. The recent trend toward youthful political leadership has now entered the American scene. It is occasional and it serves a good purpose. However, a thorough study of governmental and international leadership indicates that through the decades the people have wanted mature and experienced leadership.

In church leadership, seniority has been a real asset. Like government, modern evangelical denominations have had their interesting periods of youthful guidance. However, in the serious spiritual matters of life most groups look toward a leadership which is experienced and mature. The dominant local church and denominational leaders of our day are in the middle years of adulthood. Those who create and stabilize the thinking of larger Christian groups are also in this age bracket. Many churches look for pastoral and staff leadership among those in their middle adult years. Churches want mature adult leadership for their ministries to children and young people, because they feel more secure in it. For these and other reasons, the dominant leadership of churches will probably remain in this middle adult age group.

The world of business and industry is also an adult world. Although we have gone through "phases" when business and industry have been infatuated with youth leadership, it has not been a perennial thing. In the 'forties and 'fifties it became sophisticated in American business and industry to employ young leadership. It was during this same period (in the early 1940's) when some corporations dismissed many of their mature workers. This later proved to be a tragic mistake. The young leadership was eager, energetic, and creative, but it did not have the consistent, mature, productive ability which the older adults had manifested. By the late 'fifties and the early 'sixties most companies had convinced themselves that there was real value in mature adult leadership.

Outstanding authorities and influential persons in the major professions have usually been middle-aged adults. These leaders have frequently been stimulated by new and creative work of young artists and professionals, but this has been the exception. The fact is, that there has always been a backlog of outstanding leadership among aged professionals as long as there have been the professions and specialized vocations.

The field of education has had some interesting transitions with reference to this age of its leadership. In the past, maturity has been a specific requirement in the field of educational leadership and teaching. In medieval times the "doctor" had to be of mature years before he was ever accepted. Senility was virtually an occupational characteristic. The professional rank system of "instructor, assistant professor, associate professor, and full professor" is based, in part, on seniority.

In more recent years the average age of educational leadership has dropped into this middle adult bracket. As in other areas (those mentioned above) there has been a contemporary interest in youthful leadership in education. This is perhaps accountable to the fact that there has been so much transition in both subject matter and educational methods recently. Also, research is being emphasized, and young men like research. However, the great teaching force still is in the thirty-five to fifty-five age bracket and will continue to be. Yet, the reduction of the compulsory retirement ages in the educational areas will almost eliminate the "old sages" in active teaching.

It can be seen therefore that this is an adult-led world in almost every area. Is this also true of the family? Many interesting studies of the leadership and power structure of family life have been made. The findings run all the way from the highly democratic family — such as the one portrayed in a popular book and movie of two decades ago — to the highly patriarchal family where older parental leadership was in complete control. Although fads come and go, mature family leadership is still the order of the day. In the 1930's and '40's a tendency developed in which it was acceptable for children to call their parents by their given names. Our contemporary worship of youth and the almost idolatrous attempt to regain one's youth cosmetically and in physical health, have taken from the general tendency. However, these fads and fashions come and go and by and large a middle-aged leadership makes the significant decisions in most family living.

Although the patriarchal family structure, as we have seen earlier, has about died out in the Western culture, parental authority is asserting itself. As we leave the highly permissive family climate, the middle-aged parent and the younger grandparent will perhaps exert more authority in family living. Contributing to this is the fact that adults are living longer and remaining alert and oriented much longer.

Therefore, it can be seen that the time of leadership and control is chiefly that of middle adulthood — this is still an adult-controlled world!

(2) *Middle adulthood is a period of life which still requires changes.* The very fact that this is thought of as the productive years of the life span indicates that it is one of activity. Although there is the danger of the later adult becoming crystallized in his thinking, the middle-aged adult is still adaptable. One writer thinks of this period as being that of both achievement and conservation, while another calls it "virescence and melloescence." These, of course, come prior to "senescence."

Just as adolescence, we have discovered, is a time of decision, so the middle adult years require decision-making and changes. Many of the great issues of family living come at this time — college and marriage of the children; whether or not the middle-aged wife will begin working to occupy some of her time; new business opportunities for the husband; and decisions with reference to children or grandchildren. This calls for much self-discipline and adaptation. There are about six ways of adult growth which help in this plastic, decision-making time. They are:

a. *A help for fluid and changing adulthood is self-understanding.* It is interesting that one emphasizes a constant self-evaluation for younger people but forgets it for the adult. A constant personal inventory by the middle-aged adult is certainly essential to good mental health. Some of our "middle-aged disillusionment" might be reduced, if more adults would honestly take stock of themselves. Self-understanding would clarify the things for which we have worked, and the issues in life which personally satisfy. No doubt, such a personal study would cause many middle-aged adults to cut out some non-essentials from their life schedules. This will be discussed later in this chapter.

The good adolescent trait of "facing facts" would help many to control worry. In addition, self-understanding will often set up a new program of action (the sort of thing many rigid adults really need.) Self-evaluation also helps the maturing person to master his moods. Many times the fifty- to fifty-five-year-old adult is the one who begins to develop emotional moods and preoccupations.

b. *Self-management and self-control also aids the adult.* The middle adult many times has to begin some personal controls. If he is able to do this it is a real sign of his adult maturity. These self-controls may be in the areas of providing enough exercise for his health, limiting his diet, controlling his conversations so that he will not become too talkative, and constantly rescheduling his life as the changes come and go.

His conversational self-control cannot be exaggerated at this period, since it is very typical. In the late forties and early fifties, many adults become extremely verbose. If this verbosity is not controlled, they will probably end up to be nagging and aggravating seniles. It is interesting that over-conversation is often symptomatic of the later years of life (whereas, in the earlier years, conversation and dialogue have been encouraged in family living, many times it can become a real problem for the older adult). Many younger persons become hostile to the constant conversation and interrogation of older family members.

c. *The middle-aged adult should constantly do and learn new things.* If he tries to go through this changing period of life without accepting new ways to handle the situations and without creating new perspectives he will become frustrated. There will be almost as much new learning for an alert adult as there will be for a teen-ager. This would involve participating in new types of activities and making new friends constantly. The father who preaches this to his son often fails to practice it himself. Related to this need for new experiences, Dr. Paul B. Maves writes, "The major questions of this period of life are these: Will this person be able to continue to expand interests and knowledge? Will he be increasingly effective as a person? Will he be able to be increasingly productive? Or will he stagnate and constrict himself as a person?"[2]

d. *Another help in the middle years is learning to live with handicaps.* During this period of human development physical difficulties begin to appear. For certain middle-aged ailments correction is necessary. Others demand a constant remedial program such as taking of medicine or a certain kind of exercise. These first steps toward old age need to be accepted in a healthy way by the middle-aged adult. Adjusting to them and learning how to live with them will be the right preparation for senescence. However, some middle-aged adults find it very difficult to fit in these new responsibilities with the changing pattern of adult life. The successful business man of fifty-five feels encroached upon by the need for reducing his schedule and leaving out some activities because of health. Yet, his ability to do this verifies his maturity. As one sage said, "One has enjoyed the first two 'R's' — romance and rent, now he must adjust to the third one: rheumatism!"

Maves suggests, "All of us have to adjust to the physiological changes which are taking place within us as a result of the process of biological aging. Probably the first of these changes, of which we are aware, is that of decreasing strength,

[2] Paul B. Maves, *Understanding Ourselves as Adults* (New York: Abingdon Press, 1959), p. 146.

the slowing of recreation time, and the lessened amount of energy which we have to expend. Less obvious, but just as real is the lessening of the homeostatic capacity or the capacity to maintain an internal equilibrium and to recover from fatigue, strain, and illness which results in longer convalescent periods. Next we may become aware of some loss of sensory capacity when we begin to wear glasses or when we change to bifocals in the forties."[3]

(3) *This is a time when changes are more difficult.* As one matures these self-alterations are more difficult, of course. The middle-aged adults stand at the crossroads here. Dr. Robert L. Sutherland, director of the Hogg Foundation for Mental Health of the University of Texas, in an address suggested that middle adults should change when:

a. He begins to resist change.
b. He gets most of his satisfaction out of a minor virtue, like orderliness.
c. He represents the other extreme — if he is a disorganizer, an unorganizer, and if he clings to disarray.
d. He does well the work of the day but resists and resents evaluation.
e. He spends much of the time rejecting the government, the Republicans, the Democrats, his boss, his job, his community, his competitor.
f. He is a worrier.
g. He is a sarcastic soul.
h. He is a nagger (a recording of his voice might make him horrified at his own tenseness, unattractive manner, and authoritarian air, but he is likely to repeat the same manner the next day).
i. His feelings are hurt too easily, but he continues to look for chances to be hurt.

In 1925, E. L. Thorndike, of Columbia University, with his associates and students, began to study the learning abilities

[3] *Ibid.*, p. 137.

of adults. At the meeting of the American Association for Adult Education held in Cleveland, in 1927, he presented the results of this research. His experiments compared persons thirty-five years old and over (the average age was forty-two), with persons twenty to twenty-four years old (average age twenty-two), in their ability to learn acts of skill and to acquire various forms of knowledge.

The study, made under the most rigid of research conditions, demonstrated among others the following facts:

a. In manual skills, such as learning to write with the wrong hand, there was equal improvement in quality of legibility.

b. Both groups learned faster than they would have learned the same things as children at the age of twelve.

c. After twenty-five the decrease in learning ability is very slight — only about one per cent a year until about forty-five.

d. Any adult below forty-five is better able to learn than ages ten to fourteen. Failure to learn is not inability due to age, but is due to one or more of the following causes: always has lacked ability to learn that particular thing; desire is not strong enough to bring about proper attention; ways and means adopted inadequate and would be at any age, to that thing; and habits, ideas or tendencies which he is unwilling to alter. These interefere with the new acquisition.

Later investigations make it appear probable that the decline in ability to learn from forty-five to seventy is not much more rapid than this decline from twenty-five to forty-five. A man of sixty-five may expect to learn at least half as much per hour as he could at twenty-five and more than he could at eight or ten.

This is helped by the *experiences adults are having*. But experiences do not become educational until they have been interpreted and related to accept life philosophy. To read and study is not educational unless it helps an adult pupil to interpret the experiences he is having.

With the acceptance of these facts indicating that an adult can make changes (in family living or elsewhere) then, what helps are there? How can an adult change? Perhaps, the following are workable:

1. Know what is needed to be changed. Self-insight does not come easily.

2. Take a half-step backward (this is added as a word of caution). Some persons, as they try to improve themselves for the better, become overly burdened with a sense of guilt, of inadequacy, and of mistakes in the past. Avoid this whenever possible.

3. The most important single factor in successful change consists in using one's intelligence to discover a new way of behaving which is more emotionally satisfying than the old.

4. If one associates with others (who represent to him the best personality traits) he automatically achieves some of their better ways of living.

5. If, through these earlier steps, a person comes to know himself moderately well, then he can judge his own progress.

6. One can change in particulars more easily if he acquires appropriate basic attitudes such as open-mindedness, a belief in the goodness of human nature, and a faith in the future.

Religionists and educators have long talked in these terms, but more recently industrialists, themselves, are discovering that in the least of us there is a spark of nobility. Most of us not only can rise above the motive of intelligent selfishness to a higher order of living, if encouraged, but we yearn to do so.

Change has always been related to happiness and fulfillment at any age.

MIDDLE ADULTS AVOIDING REALITIES

Modern adults are attempting to avoid the difficulties of life. Adults are using preoccupation, social acceptance, a passion for making money, and leisure time as means of avoiding the realities of life. These immature people (some of them in their sixties) want to avoid the issues of life and try to live without difficulties. Overprotected people never mature.

Some adults try to make it easy on themselves by just not making decisions. They ignore some of the main issues in life. For example, some adults live as though God did not exist. Most of the adults who were not in Sunday school last Sunday did not get up at 6:00 A.M. and study the pros and cons of Sunday school attendance and then about 9:00 A.M. "decide" not to attend. Most of the people not in attendance never thought about Sunday school. They simply ignore spiritual matters. Their sin (greater than disobeying God) is the flagrant sin of ignoring God.

There is a danger of our becoming a generation of people who are afraid to face up to issues. A study of the struggles and triumphs of biblical characters is helpful — although we usually recommend this to young people. All people undergo difficulties. The Bible offers real and dramatic examples of individuals who surmounted tremendous obstacles. It is profitable reading for the adult too. One can hardly say that the study of men and women in the Bible is the most "wasted hour of the week."

Most middle-aged adults need to know how people have faced up to life with God's help. They also must see how people tried to confront life without God. Thousands of older adults today could profit by a careful study of the experiences of the prodigal son, for example. They would be helped in a discussion (with other people of their own age) of the trials and adjustments made by Moses. Too many people today are looking for a protective wall around their lives. James wrote: "A double minded man is unstable in all his ways" (1:8). Bible study can help the "double minded" adult face up to issues and handle them!

Too often the middle-aged adult becomes preoccupied with things which really take from the rich possibilities of life. He avoids realities by this preoccupation with secondary things. What are some of these secondary things?

(1) Preoccupation With Vocation

Rather than face up to the responsibilities of keeping his marriage vital and meaningful, some adult men devote themselves completely to business. They may have lost the communicative skills needed to engage in meaningful dialogue with wife or child. Thus, it is easier to retreat to the world of business or profession. Often business successes substitute psychologically for failure in family living.

For these reasons too much "small talk" takes place in marriages of the middle years. The day will come — only too soon — when the husband will be retired from business. If not, he may be incapacitated. Then the real communication between older husband and wife will be next to communication with God in importance.

Remember, the middle-aged wife may face some of these problem situations too. Many of the one out of four working mothers are in this age group. Working preoccupation may plague them too.[4]

(2) Preoccupation With Children and Grandchildren

Often the middle-aged adult still has children at home (secondary school or in a local college) and fails to communicate with her husband with much depth. God intended

---

[4] For a further discussion read Dorothy Whyte Cotton's (Edtor-in-chief of *Parents* magazine) "The Case for the Working Mother," published recently by Stein and Day. She discusses psychological pressures from husbands, neighbors, relatives, and guilt feelings related to working women.

that this interest in children would shift back to mate when the children matured.

Sometimes this is even the prologue to preoccupation in the grandchildren. Thus, a discussion of the middle-aged adult and his grandchildren is in order here.

Somewhere between young adulthood and senility there is, for many, the wonderful land of "grandparenthood." It can provide some of the most satisfying and fulfilling family experiences. It is a second chance at procreation — symbolic and not actual this time. Yet, it can be as enjoyable as parenthood was.

With our present life span, God enables many to see two, or even three, generations of offspring. Having one's children and grandchildren around him gives a patriarchal satisfaction that is real. It exemplifies the "family" in the fullest sense. One is reminded of the eldest male surveying his clan or tribe in the days of the ancient Hebrews. He was so proud! God speaks, in His Word, of these merited satisfactions.

With this "second parenthood" comes a repetition of some old problems, however. Even as the parent must be careful not to "spoil" the child, so must grandparents fight this temptation.

Where mother, with over-attention to a child, would be faced with a jealous husband, grandparents' over-attentiveness to grandchildren can bring a similar response from parents. The two older generations might also disagree as to the training and guidance of the child. In other cases young fathers resent domination by mothers-in-law. The daughters are caught in between. The initial family circle is broken when grandparents break the "trinity of being" as Brunner uses the phrase. The trinity includes father, mother, and child.

Perhaps, the best rules for grandparents are comparable to the following:

1. A generation and its children constitute the initial family. It, as a separate unit, is responsible for its own management. Other relatives — even grandparents — should always play only a secondary role.

2. Therefore, the children must be the primary responsibility (in every way) of their own parents. Outside help must be secondary and minimal.

3. Three and even four generations have lived happily together in other cultures. However, this does not seem to be desirable in our American culture.

4. Children should have more contacts with their own parents than with grandparents or any other relatives.

5. Parents should be wise enough to draw on the experience of their own parents and "ask for" help in rearing children. Only on this invitation should grandparents offer help. Exceptions would be in cases of parental mistreatment of children, of course.

6. Grandparents should give to grandchildren through or with parents — even children understand "channels" and "authority."

7. Grandparents should "baby sit" with the children only enough for healthy emotional contact. It should not become commonplace for the children nor a chore for the grandparents. Thus, it is advisable for parents to have other baby-sitters on call to supplement.

8. Both generations should hold up each other before the children. Differences should be solved away from the youngsters.

9. Grandparents themselves (not parents) should control "over-fixations" toward themselves from grandchildren. If parents have to suggest that grandparents are over-attentive, harm will always be done.

10. Every family member has a unique and significant part to play. Each must understand his "job description"

and avoid "over-lapping." Grandparents should enjoy their role and not try to usurp the parents' role!

The family is an interesting configuration. No two persons in the pattern are the same. No two positions are alike. No family member can be more significant than another. God gives each the opportunity to play each developing part: the child, the teenager, the newly married, the parent, the adult, the grandparent, the retired one. As one reaches each of these developmental levels, he ought to achieve the tasks of each to the best of his ability. Then he really enjoys each succeeding one. He doesn't have to regress to a prior level to "relive" it.

Acceptance of the above would reduce the number of grandmothers who want to be "mother again"!

Thus, the parent who fails to focus his or her major attention on life's mate, when the children can handle themselves, is cheating his own marriage.

This resumption of married focus on one's partner can be a beautiful thing. Middle adults must make special, yet subtle, efforts to smoothly achieve this shift. Sometimes this possible communication problem calls for new dialogical means to enable barriers of language, purposes, anxieties, concepts, and images to be handled.

Whereas, earlier focus of concentration was on children as the major emphasis and one another as a minor emphasis, now the marriage partner must have major attention with that of children secondary.

(3) *Preoccupation With Social Life*

Frequently, the adult in his middle years has his first real opportunity for full social participation. Children do not consume so much time and effort. Vocational success may allow a little more leisure time. More participation in community and church affairs involves new friendships. These and other conditions may cause a preoccupation with social activities. Family disintegration too frequently follows.

The "social whirl" of country club, civic club, garden club, and a hundred others leave a middle-aged adult "clubbed to death." This involvement reduces real conversational opportunities between husband and wife. Only honest dialogical discussion about their real interests, mission in life, and sense of values can lead them, together, to separate the "wheat from the chaff."

Then they still have courage enough to remove the lesser of these activities and retain only the most significant. They will still be dealing with this problem in retirement!

Many middle adult couples who go for coffee after church on Sunday evening discuss the press and complexities of life. They talk about dreading the "rat race" of the coming week. They dream about simple life on the farm, or at the seashore, or in the mountains. Yet, too few do anything about the situation until retirement.

Over-activity brings on preoccuption. Preoccupation brings on less conversation!

Incidentally, another issue this age group in family living faces is that of social and recreational life with those of the same sex group. Men need some fellowship with other men. Women have similar social needs. Yet this must not so dominate the situation that married couples are kept apart too much. During these years when the family reduces in numbers, these adults need each other.

(4) *Preoccupation With Self and Physical Restoration*

Our culture is one of the few in history which worships youth. Many psychological reactions to this play on the family. This abnormal fear of the aging process has caused a fear of the later years. It also has prompted men and women to employ all sorts of "restorative" acts when they reach the middle years.

This preoccupation with cosmetic and phyiscal restoration not only consumes much of some middle adults' time, but more significantly their interest. The emotional reactions to this artificial focus of attention are many. Some adults react to it by neglecting household duties, husband, and serious responsibilities such as church and community service. In addition, the adult becomes self-conscious. She wonders if people really think she looks younger and more attractive. Is the time, money, patience, and energy worth it all! He or she may unconsciously resort to immature behavior and silliness to build this image of the younger person. This tends to become exaggerated and the adult, thus unwillingly, hurts his social contacts. He or she becomes "that old fool" who acts like a "kid."

What a tragedy for the natural maturity of adulthood to be covered over with this artificial attempt at youth. How significant it is for adults to "act their age"! Otherwise this self-consciousness harms the natural extroversion of personality.

More tragic is the husband (or wife) who becomes secondary in importance to the beauty salon, diet, and restoration schedule. This preoccupation is, no doubt, causal to the increase in middle adult separations, estrangements, and divorces.

Billy Rose once said that he felt the most beautiful women and the most handsome men were those in their middle adult years. Others agree that true beauty and stature requires some aging and maturing. Too many adults fret because their children wanted to grow up too fast and wouldn't enjoy each age to the fullest. These same adults violate their own advice. They don't enjoy each God-given age as it comes. "Growing old together" feeds the dialogical freedom of marriage. To fight maturity is to defy God.

Another reaction to this artificiating has to do with the other marriage partner. That is, if one emphasizes youth and restoration to an exaggerated degree, he or she has a tendency to look down on his partner. A couple should decide together about such practices and activities.

I know a middle-aged adult couple who are both young in body and spirit by nature. They and their two teenaged sons take exercises together, go skiing at Christmas, and involve themselves in "total family" hobbies only. These two parents, needless to say, stay young in appearance and attitude. This is genuine youth — not artificial and cosmetic!

Many more preoccupations keep middle-aged adults from facing the realities of their lives. They take care of the young and the old and really need to spend more time thinking about their present and future relationships with each other. One newspaper writer said recently that they are the "overlooked generation." He said that middle-aged adults do most of the work, keep the pocket books, and see that things are kept running in general. He suggests a salute to them!

THE MIDDLE-AGED ADULT ALONE

The prior discussion has been predicated on the presence of a marriage partner. Yet many lose life companions during this period. This leaves the "family of one" as mentioned in the following chapter and also early in this book. The adult alone can live a rich and fulfilled life. Children and grandchildren can fill needs. The church can supplement family roles psychologically as well as spiritually. The maturity and experience of the single, middle-aged adult enables him to serve church, community and welfare in a constructive way.

Instead of an unnecessary "moonlighting job" this adult can use his spare time helping others and giving meaningful assistance to needy family members. To keep his mental health he should:

1. Acquire the habit of facing facts
2. Learn to evaluate himself

3. Learn to control worry
4. Have a program of action
5. Master his moods
6. Learn to deal with handicaps
7. Get along with others

Someone said that this age is between juvenile delinquency and senior citizenship and one has to take care of himself!

Self-sufficiency is needed — yet, not to the point of unhealthy independence.

The needs of single, middle-aged adults are similar to those of younger adults as given in chapter 1. They were: *they must be wanted and needed; they should be creative and busy; and they need to belong to the fellowship.*

In conclusion, the rich, mature communion of souls, who have run the gamuts of all levels of communication, is a true reward. These mature ones are tired of the eager, sophisticated conversation of young adulthood. (This grew out of their "know-it-all" adolescent period.) They weary of the business and club talk of the young adult years.

Now, there is a reverting back to simple conversation — almost like childhood: "Good, plain questions and good, plain answers!"

The satisfactions of sharing one's experiences make finding someone to listen the only problem. Life has taken in so much — *now much must be released.*

Conversation may, therefore, become ego-centric. Family members and friends must continually encourage *exchange of ideas* in conversation with the middle-aged adult. He must be led to have new interests in other people and their experiences. This "commerce" of conversation assists mental and social health and staves off the lack of conversation in old age.

Man, "God's talking image," grows spiritually, emotionally, intellectually, and socially by exercising the aptitude and skill of conversation. There is no more significant climate for this dialogue than the family of two — in the prime of the "middle years"!

7. The Later Years

"... monologue — the silent spot"

WHAT ABOUT THE LATER YEARS — the "Golden" years of family life? We have looked at every other period of life in the home and family. The children have married or entered into the career life of the single adult. Mother and father now begin the "second honeymoon."

How do you feel about retirement? Many Americans dread it! However, it can be life's richest period of family living. These later years may find the "family" in the form of mother and father alone again. The mature dialogue of the productive years, as discussed in the last chapter, now becomes richer. Age now brings an increased help for each other — meeting new physical and emotional needs. This deepens love and devotion. In turn, conversation, although less verbose, may be more meaningful.

The one "little smile of love" between an older husband and wife carries more meaning now than it did fifty years prior during engagement. The press of each other's hand communicates volumes of real dialogue.

Then, the retired person alone constitutes a family also. These "families of one" need the same satisfactions, yet in other forms. Such satisfactions were made to be anticipated by man — not dreaded!

We have minimized these joys and exaggerated the handicaps and fears. Yet, the Bible says:

> What man is he that desireth life, and loveth many days, that he may see good?
> Keep thy tongue from evil, and thy lips from speaking guile.
> Depart from evil, and do good; seek peace, and pursue it.
> The eyes of the Lord are upon the righteous, and his ears are open unto their cry.
> The face of the Lord is against them that do evil, to cut off the remembrance of them from the earth.
> — PSALM 34:12-16

What are you doing (spiritually, emotionally, and economically) to prepare for your days of retirement? What part can the church play in the later years of your life? Do you think many people take into consideration the place of spiritual security and the role of Christian friends during the sunset days of this life?

Every Christian adult ought to ask himself questions like these and begin in Christian stewardship to prepare for the *whole* life span. Only as one sees the total sweep of this life as it unfolds step by step will he be ready to approach the "golden years." Dr. Karl Stolz in his book *Making the Most of the Rest of Life*[1] says that adulthood is divided into periods. They are adjustment: the twenty-fifth to the thirty-fifth year; achievement: thirty-five to fifty-five; and conservation: fifty-five to sixty-five and up. A comprehension of these developing periods of adult life will show the Christian that he must make the most of each succeeding period in

[1] Karl R. Stolz, *Making the Most of the Rest of Life* (New York: Abingdon-Cokesbury Press, 1941), pp. 28-41.

order to be ready for the final one. Life is like the dramatic build-up of a good play — each step and every scene is significant. When we do not live each period to the fullest, we are cheating ourselves of rich satisfactions. We should greatly anticipate the climax — "retirement"!

Americans, of all people in the world today, are the most concerned about retirement — sometimes to the point of anxiety. This concern has been brought about by our retirement programs in business and industry as well as by government laws. Although these measures are to give people a sense of security, they may actually cause anxiety on the part of some and take from feelings of security. The typical American dreads old age and does not look forward to it with anticipation.

We can improve the situation by beginning to build right attitudes of anticipation in the minds of our young adults.

In the following we are first going to look at right attitudes toward retirement. Then the means of preparation (which include interests, financial and vocational plans, places for retirement, friends) and a concluding discussion of the spiritual, emotional and church aspects of retirement will be discussed.

Initially, however, it will be wise to glance at some of the typical problems which aging persons face. The following listing is broad and rather inclusive. First, a typical problem is lack of security. As we shall find out, this involves many kinds of security other than financial. Second, a lack of recognition and self-esteem is a problem area for retired people. Third is a lack of new interests and stimulating situations. The older adult must adapt to and live in a changing world even as the younger person does. Too, there is a need of love and affection and many older persons are simply starved to death in this area.

This brings on a fifth problem category which is that of loneliness. Perhaps more people in later years of life are lonely than are hungry. A sixth problem area for the retired person is that of the inability to keep up. He may want to, but physical and mental handicaps may make this difficult. This presents a problem in dealing with younger people. A final problem area is that significant one of not being needed. Every human being, made in the image of God, must feel needed by his fellows. Many older people have the mistaken attitude that life has nothing else to offer. This is often brought about by lack of consideration from younger adults.

Let us now look at some of the things that can be done to solve these typical problems of the later years of life.

ATTITUDES FOR RETIREMENT

Most of us are in the category of two older gentlemen who were discussing their coming retirement. The younger of the two asked his friend, who was beginning retirement, what he planned to do the first year. The older man answered that he was going to get a rocking chair and put it on the front porch. Then the younger continued to question and asked, "What are your plans for the second year?" The older man answered with a wry grin, "Then I'll start rocking!" This attitude is typical of many of us. We are influenced by the popular poem of recent years:

> How do I know my youth has been spent?
> Because my get-up and go, got up and went.
> But, in spite of all that, I am able to grin,
> When I think where my get-up and go has been.

> Old age is golden, I have heard it said,
> But, sometimes, I wonder, as I go to bed,
> My ears in a drawer, my teeth in a cup,
> My eyes on the table until I wake up.

> Ere sleep dims my eyes, I say to myself
> Is there anything else I should lay on the shelf?
> And I am happy to say, as I close my door,
> My friends are the same as in days of yore.

When I was young, my slippers were red,
I could kick my heels right over my head.
When I grew older, my slippers were blue;
But, I still could dance the whole night through.

Now I'm old, my slippers are black
I walk to the corner and puff my way back.
The reason I know my youth has been spent,
My get-up and go has got up and went.

But I really don't mind, when I think with a grin,
Of all the places my get-up has been.
Since I have retired from life's competition,
I busy myself with complete repetition.

I get up each morning, dust off my wits,
Pick up the paper and read the obits.
If my name is missing, I know I'm not dead,
So I eat a good breakfast and go back to bed.[2]

In the past, we have thought of the active life span as going up to the later years, with the senile period projected as some "extra life" not too related to previous living. Such a concept of old age is artificial and harmful. Thinking in terms of passive, inactive living is unhealthy at any age.

Although most cultures regard old age as the prime and rewarding period of life, these later years are not anticipated happily by us in our culture. We must remedy this situation. As has been said, government, business, and industry, which have set up the automatic age for retirement, are partly responsible for this abnormal attitude.

Of the 12 million U.S. citizens who are sixty-five and over (11% of the total population), almost one half are dependent on relatives; nearly a third rely on charity. About a fourth are still working; and only two per cent are independent.[3] Thus, our wrong attitude and poor preparation have not gotten us very far.

[2] *Wobble to My Wigwam*, Vera Minga Payne, published privately.
[3] Insurance Company findings.

MEANS OF PREPARATION

The average person must prepare for retirement in several ways.

First, he must *create interests for retirement.* One ought to begin in young adulthood to develop interests which he will gradually increase toward his maturity and retirement. Some qualifications which make retirement interests good resources are as follows.

A retirement activity must be creative and productive. Fishing as a sport would not suffice psychologically. However, if some of the fish caught were sold for income, this retirement activity might work.

Retirement activities must be personally satisfying. This means that they must not be radically different from the previous routine, yet, give variation.

Retirement activities must be active and functional. Even heaven will not be a completely passive state of being. Life must grow, unfold, and create to be satisfying. Therefore, one should *increase* these interests as his vocational work *decreases.*

One must learn (before it is too late) that the simple things are usually the most satisfying and that the later years afford the time and opportunity to enjoy them. Enjoyable activities ought to be planned with eagerness, which will make retirement preparation an active experience.

A second area of readiness is, of course, financial. Financial preparation is important. A good retirement plan should include some revenue of a current nature where the dollar value will change with the times and complement a fixed pension or annuity income. The fact that less than twenty-five per cent of the people in America over sixty-five can be classified as financially secure, is evidence enough that this is a very realistic area of preparation. However, the right attitude toward money in retirement is more important *than the money.*

Now, consider the time of retirement. One's retirement program ought not begin with a calendar date — the reaching of a sixtieth or sixty-fifth birthday. It should really begin as early as possible so that one's life may go through successive changes toward that end. There are two types of retirement situations.

(1) The person employed by someone other than himself is in one position. He must cultivate an avocational activity which will become his full-time activity in retirement. This function must be something productive, creative, and satisfying. It needs to be more than just a sport or a hobby. Also, it should, in some way, be related to the type and mode of his life work. As the individual matures, he increases interest in this activity and decreases the tension involved in his full-time vocational work. Therefore, when the retirement date comes, the transition to this avocational activity as a full-time function is easier. A person in mature years who changes his way of live overnight usually brings on an early grave.

(2) The second group includes those who are self-employed. They must develop the will power to actually reduce their life's work as they increase this avocational activity. It may cost them money, but this long range, graded program is essential.

Eventually, they should be working three-quarter time on their job, then one-half time, then one-quarter time, and thus reduce gradually to retirement. All the time the retirement function has been increased at the same ratio. Only as we gear our working lives to such a program can we enter into retirement interests successfully.

PLACES FOR RETIREMENT

A discussion of the location for retirement has been held off until now because it has been exaggerated in importance.

While many people plan ahead about the *place* of retirement, they should have been thinking more about attitudes, emotional, social, and spiritual preparation. These are more significant. What value is it to be in a beautiful place if one is unhappy, friendless, or insecure? The place is not that important. The person and his fulfillment is more important.

Some test questions, relative to location, might be:

1) Do I "feel good" in the place?

2) Am I familiar with the locale — have I tested it previously on vacations and visits?

3) Are there friends whom I already know and do I have assurance that they are "my kind of folks" with my convictions and interests? (This is important since my wife or husband may precede me in death and these people may be my only "family of friends.")

4) Is the climate and the geography good for my health and habits now? Will it still be when I am older, and perhaps feeble?

5) Are there constructive work opportunities available for me? Are there facilities and companions for the continuance of avocations, interests, and hobbies?

6) What about spiritual provisions: churches, friends, and religious activities for my continued spiritual growth? Real basic security comes from these resources. Also, one's faith will enable him to make new friends with common concerns. Can the fellowship of a church be most meaningful when I am older?

7) What is the cost of living — as I shall be living? Is my information based on rumor or is it factual? Is it a hard place in which to reduce my standard of living or will I be tempted to "keep up with the Joneses"? Am I really familiar with insurance costs and taxes there? What are the local predictions, economically, for the future?

8) If I were limited in strength and activity, could I be happy and contented there?

9) Is it the locale for the expression of activities and habits to which I am accustomed or just for those I *think* I might like?

10) Are there cultural and social groups and activities which will be satisfying and stimulating to me?

11) Is good medical service available?

12) Is the place accessible? Can I easily get around when I can no longer drive? Can friends and family visit me with facility?

13) Is the locale near, too near, or too removed from loved ones?

14) Have I some assurance that these conditions and friends will wear well — can I live with them permanently?

Having reviewed these evaluations the family member is immediately faced with the decision of staying where he is living or moving to a new retirement locale. The test should be made on the basis of answers to questions like the above. Returning to a childhood home or a former residence calls for a second thought too. More than likely it is not really as you remember it. There may be dangers here as in the "greener pastures" of new, strange, and romantic places. Many times the older person is wise to "retire" right where he has been living.

Like retirement activities, the place ought to be at least comparable to the former one.

FRIENDS FOR RETIREMENT

Life in retirement must have a focal point of love and interest. Life in the later years needs to be "living that is goalward." We feel sorry for a young person who does not know friends with the same goals — but how pitiful is the older person in such a situation! Friends with common interests are needed. But the older person must continue to *feed* friendships. He must fight the typical handicaps of an older person. Somebody offered the following prayer and we shall let him (or her) remain forever anonymous:

> Lord, Thou knowest better than I know that I am growing older, will some day be old,
>
> Keep me from getting talkative, and particularly from the fatal habit of thinking I must say something on every subject and every occasion.
>
> Release me from craving to try to straighten out everybody's affairs,
>
> Make me thoughtful, but not moody, helpful but not bossy. With my vast store of wisdom it seems a pity not to use it all, but Thou knowest, Lord, that I want a few friends at the end of life.
>
> Keep my mind free from the recital of endless details, give me wings to get to the point.
>
> Seal my lips on my aches and pains. They are increasing and my love of rehearsing them is becoming sweeter as the years go by.
>
> I ask for grace enough to listen to the tales of others' pains. Help me endure them patiently.
>
> Teach me the glorious lesson that occasionally it is possible that I may be mistaken.
>
> Keep me reasonably sweet; I do not want to be a saint, some are hard to live with, but a sour old person is one of the crowning works of the devil.
>
> Help me to exact all possible fun out of life. There are so many funny things around us and I don't want to miss any of them. Amen.
>
> — *Anonymous*

Often, the key to the social contacts of older people lies in a good recreational schedule. Recreational and hobby activities which involve other people are best, of course, as means of social contact. Frequently the hobby isolates the older person. This is not best unless he has other hobbies which do involve people.

Some good tests of recreation and hobbies for the retired person might be:

1) Have I prepared for this activity — has there been a tested, growing interest?
2) Is it creative? Is my creativity expressed best in collecting, manufacturing, rearranging? Does it need reward and praise, or personal satisfaction, or competition, or usefulness?
3) Should it be, for me, best expressed indoors or outdoors? How does this fit in with the climate and geography of my retirement place?
4) Am I physically and emotionally fitted for it?
5) Does it relate well with the rest of my life schedule?
6) Is it productive? Does something worthwhile result from it?
7) Can I afford it?

The opportunities for activities which will be personally satisfying and also create friendships are unlimited. For example, some are:

1) Serve on church committees
2) Work in a church library
3) Keep the church guest register
4) Entertain special groups such as soldiers and students
5) Write historical articles about the town or various institutions
6) Roll bandages
7) Compile unique recipe books
8) Baby-sit
9) Make inventory of Senior Citizens in the community
10) Take part in community drives, such as cancer, heart, polio, etc.
11) Make costumes for church and school dramatics
12) Visit shut-ins

13) Read to blind or shut-in persons
14) Plan a half-hour of music in the evening for nursing homes
15) Arrange for book carts stocked with books, games, puzzles, and pictures for distribution in hospitals and homes
16) Make things for children
17) Work out details with nursing home operators to provide boxes of food and other items
18) Play games with shut-ins
19) Teach knitting or crocheting in institutions
20) Teach hobbies to those in homes
21) Arrange for reading machines
22) Acquaint bed patients with reflectors for reading on ceiling
23) Collect magazines for various groups—children, aged, and ill
24) Provide library service to homes
25) Aid with Goodwill Centers
26) Take blind children on rides
27) Plan activities of TB and other patients such as rides, refreshments and games
28) Fix things for friends and neighbors
29) Make choir robes for the church
30) Plan "Person to Person" programs with other groups
31) Serve as traffic policeman at schools
32) Get out of the house with a friend by visiting and seeking to make new neighbors part of the community
33) Plan a tea or coffee hour in homes with certain oldsters as hostesses who may invite their friends
34) Help with church or school mailings
35) Build or supply a place for puzzles, games, and books in nursing homes or churches

Conclusion

We have seen that the most significant thing for the younger adult is the right attitude as he looks forward to his retirement years. Then, we have discovered that there are some practical helps in setting up one's retirement program. It has been evidenced in the discussion that the most significant things are really not economic and financial, but rather spiritual, emotional, and social. In our final discussion we learn that there were certain ways in which these social, emotional, and spiritual satisfactions could be accomplished. In each of these we saw how the church can provide the right kind of friendships and the right atmosphere. One of the nation's leading authorities on retirement has, in his popular book in the field, suggested that a church provides the best social atmosphere for a person or couple during the retirement years. In a recent newspaper article the chairman of the United States Committee on Aging Geriatrics, gives a report. In it is a list of the places in which people in retirement can find friends and where they can best actively seek them out. In his list of places he puts churches first.

Both of the above authorities are secular — not necessarily religious — writers. Yet they agree that a church can provide the right friends for the person who is living in this significant period of life.

Therefore, each Christian adult should ask himself questions such as these: Am I serving in my church *now* in such ways that I will be able to actively continue when I am older? Does my Christian service (along with other wholesome and productive activities) play a significant part in my life? Can it gradually take over the majority of my time? Am I so living in Christ that when I get to the place where I must cut down on my schedule, I will still have the feeling of security in my Saviour and in the remembrance of my productive years of stewardship? Do I make such a contribution to the lives of Christians about me that were it wise for me to move to a new location later on, I would be able to make good friends in Christ wherever I am? Shall I have already lived before God in my youth, so that in the years of my maturity my life will be stimulating to the young people around about me?

Let us all work to the end that we can give satisfactory answers to such questions.

8. Divorce

". . . communication ceases"

A fascinating and helpful volume, *Divorce Problems Handbook*, states, "Divorce is the most crucial maladjustment affecting the American family today, with the number of divorce decrees being granted by our courts showing a steady increase annually." [1]

If it is "the most crucial maladjustment," then strategic moral leaders should all be concerned, informed, and feel responsible about it. Teachers of children and young people must find a real stewardship in laying foundations for permanent marriages. Marriage partners should understand the many facets of divorce and seek earnestly to keep their marriage healthy.

The following discussion will be very brief, but will survey the situation.

AN ADMISSION OF FAILURE

Without appearing harsh, one must state as a fact that divorce indicates failure on the part of one or more. The

[1] Frederick M. Kall and Harry A. Frumess, *Divorce Problems Handbook* (New York: Frederick Fell, Inc., 1961), p. XI.

failure aspect of divorce must be repeated and broadcasted, so as to combat the growing acceptance of divorce. Elton Trueblood suggests that divorce must always be an admission of failure in one of life's most sacred undertakings. Divorce is bad, it is sometimes better, however, than remaining together.

Divorce, compared with other family relations, is also conditioned by dialogue and communication. Studies show a growing break in interpersonal relations as a build-up to separation. Deep and sincere dialogue can often repair this separation. Any marriage counselor, minister, or attorney seeks to rebuild communication between a separating couple.

Estrangement in communication breeds guilt. Thus, legal experts are currently concerned over the growing employment of accusing guilt in divorce proceedings. The Interprofessional Commission, sponsored by the American Bar Association, stated that basing a divorce on guilt and punishment have proven harmful and dangerous to any future stability.

Therefore, some stigma of failure should be attached to divorce, but guilt feelings and charges of guilt (for filing divorce decrees) should probably be reduced. The approximately thirty-five different grounds for divorce in most states carry some "guilt aspect" except one: religious differences.

It is obvious that husbands and wives facing growing differences will think about eventual divorce as a possible outcome. If they are at all familiar with the legal aspects of divorce, they will contemplate divorce grounds. This leads to listing the faults and guilts of one's mate. In turn, this accelerates the break between the two and kills communication. It becomes a vicious circle.

One prominent divorce judge suggests that legal "counsel"

should be just that. [2] He believes that our situation cannot be improved until the legal profession sees the counseling and therapeutic aspects and possibilities of its work.

In summary, divorce must clearly indicate failure, but failure calls for a new start and repair — not obsessive guilt. Too, communication can correct a growing break in a marriage.

Evidence of divorce as failure — at least in America, is indicated by its growth. The knowledgeable person of our day knows that there is an increase in the number of divorces. He may not be able to quote statistics to verify this conclusion. In fact, the figures are increasing so rapidly that he could not keep up with them. One report suggests that one out of each four marriages will end in divorce or legal separation. This is immediately followed by another indicating that the incidence of divorce is one out of three marriages. Also, Brandt and Dowdy suggest that many more marriages are "psychologically broken." That is, the couple still lives under one roof, but there is no compatibility.

These "emotional divorce" types of marriages are particularly difficult for any children that are in the home. Although the marriage is kept legally together for the sake of the children such emotional climate may be worse for them than living in a better relationship with one parent. As long as this fracture in the love and marriage relationship is evident the child can never find the security he needs.

Since unfaithfulness and promiscuity may be related to a divorce situation, the whole area of morality is related to the problem. The famous sociologist, Petirim A. Sorokin, who coined the phrase "sexual revolution," suggests that this moral laxness is reflected in the growing divorce and separation rates.

[2] Reports of the American Bar Association, LXXXI (1956), p. 326 (not copyrighted).

Elton Trueblood suggests that "priority" is the chief question in this whole issue. He says that until we place high priorities on the significance of marriage as a permanent relationship, we cannot hope to improve the current situation. He adds that as marriage becomes less sacred and divorce more acceptable, many conclude that divorce is justified. [3]

A report of the millions paid annually in alimony payments is astounding. The large number of divorced women in business, industry and public school teaching grows each year.

In summary, everything indicates that we are faced with a growing situation which, for many, is a problem. Parents and teachers have many divorced persons in their families and classes. Ministering to their needs can be a very fruitful and needed service.

One of the first things needed is a change in attitudes toward divorce. This is difficult for many of us, but apparently it must come. Our problem is to retain our basic, biblical principles and yet accommodate to the needs of the present situation.

A CHANGED ATTITUDE

In discussing our current moral revolution Dr. John W. Drakeford writes that "Permissive cultures have remained at their lower level of development largely because of lack of sexual discipline. The very attitudes toward sex, seen by some as an indication of a society's foolishness, may really be an evidence of its collective wisdom." [4] Continuing to justify our established morality, Drakeford discusses the need for honestly facing all of these related problems. Divorce is one of them. Most Christians are changing their attitudes toward divorce. Dr. W. Perry Crouch says that we have no Scripture passage which would indicate divorce as an unforgivable sin.

[3] Address by Dr. Elton Trueblood, Leakey, Texas, 1962.
[4] Drakeford, John W., *The Great Sex Swindle* (Nashville: Broadman, 1966).

Divorce is a reality, and beyond human repair. Divorced persons need the ministry and love of the churches.

Attitudes have also changed from spiritual values to secular ones. This has brought about a purposelessness and meaninglessness that plagues marriage. Wallace Denton says, "There is a real need for 'meaning' in married life." Yet, this depth requires emphasis on spiritual rather than material things — this is our problem. [5]

We must change from our preoccupations with secular and material things or we can never build right attitudes toward marriage and the family. This growing preoccupation with other things is one of the real causes of divorce.

Too, the changing husband-wife roles constitute a problem. The less masculine and less responsible father vs. the less feminine, working mother breeds discontent and possible separation. There is a need for restoration of the original husband-wife roles.

One could prolong this list of changing attitudes almost indefinitely. It may be sufficient to say that our attitudes are changing and one should keep informed as best he can.

A BREACH OF VOWS

The Christian concept of marriage is one of commitment rather than legal contract. Most American citizens, nurtured in this Judeo-Christian culture, still think of marriage in this way. There are some differences in the Old Testament and the New Testament teachings on marriage and divorce, but on this commitment concept, they both agree.

A recent thesis study at Southwestern Baptist Theological Seminary concluded that since Jesus taught the "one flesh union" in marriage, this union really cannot be broken by divorce. Divorce is possible only as the recognition of a

[5] See: *What's Happening to Our Families* (Philadelphia: Westminster Press, 1963).

broken marriage relationship (due to unfaithfulness.) The Judeo-Christian pattern for marriage has been that it is more of a commitment than a contract. Elton Trueblood has some interesting things to say about this. [6]

Therefore, many Christians are looking for a less legalistic interpretation of Jesus' advice on marriage and divorce. They do not feel that the Lord forbade divorce in cases where sufficient attempts had been made to continue the marriage relationship. There are cases where all persons involved are so in conflict and in misery that life is not worth living. Sometimes there are no solutions to such marriage problems. However, these are still situations where divorce *does* break the one flesh union and this is less than the highest standard for Christian marriage. Yet many feel that this must be accepted.

One can seek to relate the Biblical teachings on man's imperfections, forgiveness, and love to his understanding of divorcees. He can be sympathetic and understanding. Deep convictions about God's giving man another chance — the "Gospel of a new beginning" will help.

Aiding divorcees to start anew, to build new friendships, to see themselves as separate families; and providing good activities for them will help. One writer believes that "Many divorces were not caused by one problem only: they are the result of meaningless life, dull, dissatisfying and monotonous boredom."

One can give meaning and sparkle to a life which will be in contrast to the dullness of a poor marriage, in his contact with divorcees.

The help which one can give to any single adults, can usually be given to divorcees. A considerable amount of new materials are available from various sources on the single adult.

[6] Trueblood, Elton and Pauline, *The Recovery of Family Life* (New York: Harper and Brothers, 1953).

Some suggestions for working with divorced persons, which are similar to methods used with all single adults, are discussed elsewhere in this volume.

MARRIAGE AGE AND DIVORCE

Some interesting studies have been made relative to age at the time of marriage and the probability of marriage success or failure. One of the classic studies was conducted by Hart and Shields in which they concluded after the study of 500 cases of marriage difficulty that if both bride and groom are under 20 years of age at the time of marriage the risk of unhappiness is 10 times as great as for marriages at later ages. [7]

Every study surveyed by this writer indicated, that for men, the best ages for marital success was over 20 years. In most cases this same age held for women, but two studies indicated that 18 or 19 years of age might be satisfactory for them.

Although age certainly doesn't determine success in marriage, it does seem to be a strong influence. It is secondary to compatibility; good personality adjustments; spiritual and philosophical common beliefs; and mutual agreements on goals and objectives. The chronological age of marriage partners seems to be a stronger determinant of success in marriage than age difference between the two marriage partners. However, not all surveys and studies agree at this point.

One must be reminded that immaturity is not only a difficulty involved in marriage at an early age, but economics are also involved. Most studies indicated that marriages of younger people are those who come from lower socio-economic backgrounds. An interesting comparison at this point is the average marriage age in America as over against Great

[7] L. M. Terman Study, *Psychological Factors in Marital Happiness,* copyright by McGraw-Hill Book.

Britain. In recent years the average marriage age in Great Britain has risen — particularly since World War II. British surveys have indicated that the average marriage age in England is approaching 30 years. This would, of course, mean that most of these people were emotionally mature. However, this must be counterbalanced with the fact that the male-female ratio in Britain has been very poor since the war.

The American education system has also had an influence as to age of marriages and therefore, indirectly, the divorce rate. Most studies of college and university students who marry indicate that they find a reasonable degree of compatibility. In addition, they almost always make better grades than single students.

Another interesting factor in marriage age is the teenage "fad!" Social psychologists have learned that as teenage fads come and go they have a definite impact on marriage age. Adolescents go through one period where it is considered the sophisticated thing to become engaged and married at a very early age. This is highly conditioned and regulated by the peer group. Other fads make it the acceptable thing to hold off marriage until formal education has been completed. It is important that teenage fads — which usually have no foundation in fact or logic — influence marriage age in America. Most studies indicate that they do have some influence.

Another interesting involvement, mentioned elsewhere in this volume, is a new psychological concept of the age of adolescence. Adolescence, incidentally, is rather our concept. Most cultures understand growth as going directly from childhood to adulthood.

Initially American scholars thought of adolescence as beginning with the twelfth year and concluding with the eighteenth year. Subsequently these scholars considered that adolescence went through the twenty-first year. It was at this time that most of our federal laws were established. More recently psychologists and sociologists think of adolescence as going through the twenty-fourth year. This concept means, of course, that adulthood does not begin until the twenty-fifth year. Almost all cultures, ancient and contemporary, see childhood as concluding with the child's twelfth year or puberty. After some rite — usually for the male child — he became an adult. He was then adult until he died. The adolescent concept is typically American and Western.

One interesting study made a number of years ago indicated that happy marriages usually resulted where the husband was from one to eight years older than the wife. One part of the same study brought forth one most unusual finding. That is, that the largest percentage of happy husbands had married *women* who were three to four years *older than they were*. If these studies were made of younger married couples, it will be remembered that the maturity level is rapidly changing in later adolescence and early adulthood. This might partially explain these findings.

Most parents, for example, are aware of the fact that prior to puberty the female matures faster than the male. However, subsequent to this time there is an accelerated development by the male.

There is no doubt that as the general public becomes advised about these changing concepts of age they will have some impact on marriage.

When spiritual, romantic, and emotional conflicts between marriage partners are of such intensity that they are open and marked, the resultant atmosphere may be the worse thing in the world for a growing child. These diseased marriages may infect children to the extent that they themselves will never understand proper marriage and family life in the future.

In fact, a recent article in a popular magazine indicated

that young divorced girls came dominantly from divorced or separated homes.

Perhaps very little advantage can come from this kind of artificially forced family relationship. Therefore, many people today consider the retention of a marriage relationship for the benefit of children as somewhat questionable. As already indicated, the criteria would depend on the emotional conflict between the parents.

Everyone knows of cases where he has said, in exasperation, "I believe it would almost be better for them to go ahead and get a divorce for the sake of the children." This kind of statement seems in contrast to the typical one which is "they certainly ought to stay together for the sake of the children." This kind of situation calls for some prayerful thinking and for considering the welfare of the young.

As we understand the home, the child who only has one parent is living in an abnormal family setting. Yet, we are familiar with many families like this where there is a wholesome, spiritual attitude and from which children have developed as mature well adjusted adults. [8] As discussed elsewhere, a single adult (in his own domicile) is considered a family. Thus, we can say — at least psychologically, that a child, or children, living with one parent does have "a family."

A similar artificial home is that of the children's institution. The children resident in our children's homes and orphanages are from broken homes — few are orphaned. Dr. R. C. Campbell, President of Buckner Baptist Benevolences in Texas, which operates the nation's largest Baptist children's home, says that approximately 98 percent of their children and adolescents come from "disrupted" families. This means divorced, estranged, deserted, or legally separated parents

[8] Brandt, Henry R. and Dowdy, Homer E., *Building a Christian Home* (Wheaton, Illinois: Scripture Press, 1960), p. 68.

are involved in these cases. Less than 2 percent of their youngsters have lost parents in death. This situation typifies the divorce problem among Baptist families as most of these children come from Baptist backgrounds (at least, nominally).

Perhaps any conclusion at this point would be relative to whether or not the cost of holding the marriage together was really worth it all. It becomes very evident that each case would have to be judged as an individual one. Whatever decision is reached, should be in the light of the admonition: Remember the children! Finally, regardless of conflicting reports on the number of divorces, real or emotional, they all indicate an increase — none shows a decline. Too, we are changing our attitudes toward this social problem. We must restudy the religious and moral implications of "one flesh," and divorce should consider the children. It is a last resort.

Appendix

THE CHURCH AND FAMILY LIFE EDUCATION

The church can assist the family in its common task. The
following helps are suggested.

(1) *Some churches have provided special programs* to help
the family. One of the first such Christian home church
emphases was held in 1946 in the state of Mississippi. It
pioneered in the inclusion of family problem conferences. A
discussion of the child in the home was led by a panel which
included: a public school leader, a psychiatrist, a sociologist,
a pastor, and a psychologist. It was a practical approach to
family life.

In such democratic and permissive situations as this,
church family life conferences have grown. They have become one of the major programming functions for a church's
annual calendar. Through the years the denominations have
offered helpful suggestions and provided materials. There
is almost no limit to the approaches to family life programs.
Each church can adapt the suggestions and materials provided to its own situation.

In evaluating some of the following programs one can see the versatility which is possible. Perhaps every church ought to vary its program from year to year. The following Christian home programs are samples of some which have been used.

A workshop in Christian family living is usually the most helpful. For example, it can begin with a family emphasis in Sunday messages and an after-church fellowship for the young people. During this period a practical discussion on courtship and marriage problems might be carried on. On Monday and Tuesday evenings special workshop periods might be held for married young people. These groups are given complete freedom of participation following some remarks by the leader. The periods should be kept of sufficient length to really solve some problems. Informality is predominant. On Tuesday morning there might be a coffee period of discussion for the mothers of nursery, beginner and cradle-roll age children. On Wednesday evening the theme might be carried on in a talk at a dinner for Bible school teachers and officers. On Thursday evening the parents of teen-agers could have their session, and on Friday night the parents of Junior children could be invited to departmental open-house and a brief talk and discussion following. On Saturday morning the adults could discuss preparation for Christian retirement at a breakfast in the church.

This is one of the first Christian family type emphases which carries the practical solution of problems as its theme all through the week. Many Christian home weeks previous to this time usually had been, in the main, inspirational in nature. This workshop and discussion method has been well received by the people and the total attendance for such weeks included representatives from most every family in the church.

Another workshop type of week could begin on Sunday with Christian home messages and continue with morning coffees and evening discussions through Thursday night. This week could be concluded with a family dedication service on Friday evening.

A brief social period should follow every discussion period both morning and evening. One night a youth panel could be used with the young people discussing Christian marriage and family living. The extensive use of the church library and a special book display should be involved in the meeting. This is a general practice now included in almost every good family emphasis.

A more extensive Christian Home Week could include all kinds of interest groups related to family living. These hobby groups in various sections of the church might last for one hour each session. These could include all sorts of interest areas related to home life, such as: food and table decorations, ceramics and needlework, interior decorating, gardening, furniture refinishing, photography, outdoor cooking, or a class in charm. Also, there are several groups relative to sports and do-it-yourself crafts possible. Altogether, there could be many such sessions going on simultaneously. Following these one might have a general assembly in the auditorium.

A home dedication service could be offered or an appropriate play given on the concluding evening. As in all marriage and family programs the leaders spend extensive time in personal counseling with the people.

It was apparent that some churches preferred to have a three- or four-day home emphasis every year, rather than a full week on alternating years or occasionally. This trend has continued to grow in many churches.

One such schedule ran Sunday through Wednesday night. On Sunday, messages were given on the Christian home and the daily programs followed this schedule: 7:00 p.m. — Hobby Hour Classes, of which there were seven groups. This number proved highly successful for a church of medium size. Then adults and married young people assembled in the lower auditorium for a message by the pastor. To add a practical note a panel or open discussion in the adult assembly was offered. Then, at 8:30 everyone came together for a coffee time. The entire evening's program was usually adjourned by 9:00 o'clock.

Another such schedule of activities includes morning, afternoon, and evening sessions varying from Monday through Thursday. Then there can be hobby groups too.

A church in Oklahoma City tried a plan which has been used by other churches with success. It had three or four one-day emphases on the Christian home throughout the year: one in the fall, one in the winter, and one in the spring. This was done in lieu of an emphasis of four to seven consecutive days in the spring. Each of these quarterly programs was for a particular age group or aspect of Christian family life.

A typical three-day Christian home emphasis can begin on Friday evening with a retreat for single young people at a resort near the city. This allows a wonderful opportunity for informal discussion. Then on Saturday morning one might have a coffee for the parents of younger children and on Saturday evening discussions for young married adults. Both Sunday services could carry a family theme. A Sunday worship service, with most of the people seated in church by families, works quite well. Another age group might meet for discussion after church that evening. Many contacts can be made within the one night and two full days and this "week-end" plan has been used with much success.

A fall Christian home emphasis, as described below, demonstrates how the schedule can be worked out in another season other than the traditional Spring months (particularly May). The meeting was held August 31 to September 3, taking advantage of the fact that the families had just returned from their summer vacations. They were well pre-

pared for the idea of better family living and a family dedication service concluded the meeting on Wednesday night
in preparation for the beginning of school and the "settled"
fall family schedule of living.

Another family life approach, such as the following, has
been used with success. The theme of the emphasis was,
"The Child in the Home," and was held for four successive
Wednesday nights. It was a discussion type program and
held in an assembly room. Although there were large groups
in attendance, discussion and problem-solving were carried
on. The sessions, "The Home and the Teen-ager"; "The
Junior"; "The Primary Child" and "The Pre-School Child,"
were used also.

A "Parents' Night" approach can also be employed. Public
school teachers, with the parents of the children of the
church, meet in the auditorium for one large group discussion. The main theme of this emphasis can be, "The Relationship of Home, Church, and School." Then "open house"
might be provided in all Sunday school departments.

One new family dedication approach in the Christian
Home Week has been developed. The families were invited
at the beginning of the final family dedication service to sit
together leaving some empty space in the pews between
families. As the hymn is played, the invitation is given for
any member of the family outside the church membership
to complete the family circle in becoming a church member.
Also, the idea of instituting or improving the Family Altar is
suggested. Dedication to better fellowship in the home is
invited. Each family is *given the opportunity to discuss such
spirtiual problems among themselves right there in the service*. On the basis of this immediate discussion, decisions are
made by the families. After the service many people say
that in such an environment they talk about things which,
somehow, they never get around to discussing at home.

Churches have done a splendid job in this whole area and

only the future will tell what new possibilities lie ahead. We must keep the vital balance of inspiration and information (people are seeking realistic answers to their family problems). Our faith *does* provide such answers.

Below are given sample outlines for such programs putting to work the practices advocated in this book:

PLAN I

Friday 7:00 p.m. Dinner for parents and workers with children, up to 12 years old

"As the Twig Is Bent"

(The discussion deals with the role of family and church in preparing the child for religious experiences. Discipline, developmental tasks, and teaching methods are related. The level to which a child must come for conversion [accountability] is defined. Open discussion follows.)

Saturday 10:00 a.m. A coffee for parents and workers with teen-agers

"The Strange Journey"

(Some revolutionary ideas are presented which show how most adults have grossly misunderstood today's teen-ager and have, thus, made mistakes in dealing with him. His real needs, guidance, his fads, his maturity are then discussed by the group.)

Saturday 7:00 p.m. All adults meet to discuss:

"Preparation for Christian Retirement"

(Attitudinal, emotional, vocational, financial, and spiritual preparation is discussed. Specific plans and programs are suggested and are built upon the thesis that preparation must begin early. The role of the church is emphasized. An open discussion concludes the session.)

Saturday 7:30 p.m. A social for teenagers has been in

progress since 7:30 p.m. At 8:30 p.m. they are led
in the discussion:

"Personality — Key to Love, Courtship, and Marriage"
(The American system of social development, meeting friends, dating, and preparation for marriage are
discussed. The ways in which the Christian tradition
is woven into this are emphasized. Comments on
teen-aged fads, stereotypes, and conditions such as
"going steady," parental control, and dating dialogue
are given. Discussion follows.)

Sunday morning worship service

Message: "Family Dedication"

The families are seated together in the service. The
invitation includes:

1. Profession of faith (with the suggestion that it might
   finish or help complete the family circle).

2. Church membership (with the suggestion that such a
   step might help complete the family in the church).

3. The family commits itself to tithe.

4. The family commits itself to family devotion daily
   (or to improve family devotion as it now stands).

5. The family commits itself to pray — as a family —
   about some problem or issue.

6. The family commits itself to specifically seek to wit-
   ness to a lost family member — not present.

7. The family publicly rededicates itself.

PLAN II

Same as Plan I, only there is a concluding Sunday evening
service. In this case, the message:

"The Bible and the Home"

is given Sunday morning and the dedication service
would take place at night.

PLAN III

Sunday morning worship service:
> "The Bible in the Home"

Sunday evening service:
> "Communism vs. The Christian Family"

After service: Refreshments and discussion for teenagers:
> "Personality — Key to Love, Courtship, and Marriage"
> (The American system of social development, meeting friends, dating, and preparation for marriage are dis--cussed. The ways in which the Christian tradition is woven into this are emphasized. Comments on teen-aged fads, stereotypes, and conditions as "going steady," parental control, and dating dialogue are given. Discussion follows.)

Monday 7:00 p.m. All adults meet to discuss:
> "Preparation for Christian Retirement"
> (Attitudinal, emotional, vocational, financial, and spiritual preparation is discussed. Specific plans and programs are suggested and are built upon the thesis that preparation must begin early. The role of the church is emphasized. An open discussion concludes the session.)

Refreshments follow

Tuesday 10:00 a.m. A coffee for parents and workers with children, up to 12 years old.
> "As the Twig Is Bent"
> (The discussion deals with the role of family and church in preparing the child for religious experiences. Discipline, developmental tasks, and teaching methods are related. The level to which a child must come for religious experiences [accountability] is defined. Open discussion follows.)

Tuesday 7:00 p.m. Conference for the single adult as a family:

"The Family of the Church"

(The role of the single or separated adult in all of its implications will be viewed. Emphasis will be given to the spiritual, social, emotional, and vocational life. Single adult developmental tasks will be analyzed. Discussion follows.)

Wednesday a.m. Coffee at 10:00 for parents and workers with teen-agers:

"The Strange Journey"

(Some revolutionary ideas are presented which show how most adults have grossly misunderstood today's teen-ager and have, thus, made mistakes in dealing with him. His real needs, guidance, his fads, his maturity are then discussed by the group.)

Wednesday 7:00 p.m. General service (same as above)

(2) In addition to these special programs, the church can *involve good principles of Christian family living in its regular curriculum.*

One major denomination, after much research and curriculum reconstruction, has done this in these areas: the place of the family in the church; the responsibility of the church in teaching the vocation of marriage and parenthood; the responsibility of the home for the Christian nurture of its members; and the ministry of the church to its families. This approach makes the church and family curriculum one and the same.

A writer of another denomination suggests that his churches accomplish this "church-home guidance" throughout the year by:

(a) Surveying community and church family needs

(b) Using denominational literature emphasizing the family more effectively

(c) Drawing help from local church institutions related

to counseling, mental health, and family life education

(d) Using the study groups of the church (Sunday school classes, youth groups, women's societies, and others) in studying Christian family life

(e) Providing more personal family counseling by church staff

(f) Magnifying family worship

(g) Using the church library for family life education

(h) Emphasizing good home life in the churches' adult programs

The objectives of Christian family life and parenthood (as suggested in the *International Curriculum Guide*) can be used as a testing scale for the church's entire program. A kind of "guidance approach" to improving the family lives of church members can be employed. This sees the church's ministry as preventive — helping family members to live well — and curative — aiding when they do have family problems. Such an approach will also:

(a) Make the church sensitive to its special Christian mission to the family

(b) Create a "family fellowship" in the church

(c) Formulate channels for ministering to family needs

(d) Constantly relate the church to its families

BIBLIOGRAPHY

Adolescents

Ausubel, David P., *Theory and Problems of Adolescent Development.* New York: Grune and Stratton, Inc., 1954.

Baruch, Dorothy W., *How to Live With Your Teen-ager.* New York: McGraw-Hill Book Company, Inc., 1953.

Bell, A. Donald, *In Christian Love: The Young Person in Ministry.* Nashville: Convention Press, 1968.

Blos, Peter, *The Adolescent Personality.* New York: Appleton-Century-Crofts, Inc., 1941.

Bossard, James H. S., *The Sociology of Child Development.* New York: Harper and Brothers, 1954.

Crawford, John E., *Better Ways of Growing Up.* Muhlenberg.

Cruickshank, William M. (ed.), *Psychology of Exceptional Children and Youth.* Englewood Cliffs, New Jersey: Prentice-Hall, Inc., 1955.

Elliott, Grace Loucks, *Understanding the Adolescent Girl.* Woman's Press.

Ernest, Clayton H., *What Shall I Be?* New York: Appleton-Century Company, 1924.

Frank, L. K., R. Harrison, E. Hellersberg, K. Machover, and M. Steiner, *Personality Development in Adolescent Girls.* New Orleans: Child Development Publications, 1953.

Gallagher, J. Roswell, and Herbert I. Harris, *Emotional Problems of Adolescents.* New York: Oxford University Press, 1958.

Gesell, Arnold, Frances L. Ilg, and Louise Bates Ames, *Youth, the Years from Ten to Sixteen.* New York: Harper and Brothers, 1956.

Gibson, Jessie E., *On Being a Girl.* New York: Macmillan Company, 1927.

Glueck, Sheldon and Eleanor, *Unraveling Juvenile Delinquency.* Commonwealth Fund.

Horrocks, John E., *The Psychology of Adolescence.* Boston: Houghton Mifflin Company, 1951.

Hurlock, Elizabeth B., *Adolescent Development.* New York: McGraw-Hill Book Company, Inc., 1955.

Josselyn, Irene M., *The Adolescent and His World.* New York: Family Service Association of America, 1952.

Kettelkamp, Gilbert C., *Teaching Adolescents.* Boston: D. C. Heath and Company, 1954.

Kuhlen, Raymond G., *The Psychology of Adolescent Development.* New York: Harper and Brothers, 1952.

Landis, Paul H., *Understanding Teen-Agers.* New York: Appleton-Century-Crofts, Inc., 1955.

Malm, Marguerite, and Olis G. Jamison, *Adolescence.* New York: McGraw-Hill Book Company, Inc., 1952.

Overton, Grace Sloan, *Living With Teeners.* Nashville: Broadman Press, 1950

Sconfeld, William, *The Stork Didn't Bring You — The Facts of Life For Teen-Agers.* Hermitage House.

Seidman, Jerome M. (ed.), *The Adolescent.* New York: The Dryden Press, Inc., 1953.

Wattenberg, William W., *The Adolescent Years.* New York: Harcourt, Brace, and Company, Inc., 1955.

Wells, Mildred White, *Youth and Your Community.* New York: Public Affairs Pamphlets, 22 E. 38th Street.

Williamson, E. G., *Counseling Adolescents.* New York: McGraw-Hill Book Company, Inc., 1950.

Wittenberg, Rudolph M., *Adolescence and Discipline.* New York: Association Press, 1959.

CHILD IN THE FAMILY

Aldrich, C. A., *Babies Are Human Beings.* Macmillan.

————, *Feeding Our Old Fashioned Children.* Macmillan.

Allen, W. Y. and D. Campbell, *The Creative Nursery Center.* Family Service Association of America.

Anderson, Dwight, *The Other Side of the Bottle.* Wynn.

Barker, Roger, *Child Behavior and Development.* McGraw-Hill.

Baruch, Dorothy W., *How to Discipline Your Children.* New York: Public Affairs Pamphlets, 22 E. 38th Street.

Bogardus, La Donna, *Christian Education of Retarded Children and Youth*. Nashville: Abingdon Press, 1963.

Breasted, J. H., *The Dawn of Conscience*. Charles Scribner's Sons, 1934.

Donnelly, Richard J., *Active Games and Contests*. New York: Ronald Press, Company, 1958.

Driscoll, Gertrude, *How to Study the Behavior of Children*. New York: Bureau of Publications, Teachers College, Columbia University.

Foshee, Howard, "Your Church and the Mentally Retarded." Nashville: Baptist Sunday School Board.

Fox, H. W., *The Child's Approach to Religion*. New York: Harper and Brothers, 1945.

Frank, Josette, *Comics, Radio, Movies — and Children*. New York: Public Affairs Pamphlets, 22 E. 38th Street.

Frank, Mary, *How to Help Your Child in School*. Viking.

Garrison, Karl C., *The Psychology of Exceptional Children*. University of Georgia, 1965.

Gesell, Arnold and F. L. Ilg., *Infant and Child in the Culture of Today*. New York: Harper, 1943.

Hymes, James L., *Enjoy Your Child — Ages 1, 2, and 3*. New York: Public Affairs Pamphlets, 22 E. 38th Street.

————, *How to Tell Your Child About Sex*. New York: Public Affairs Pamphlets, 22 E. 38th Street.

————, *Three to Six: Your Child Starts to School*. New York: Public Affairs Pamphlets, 22 E. 38th Street.

————, *Understanding Your Child*. New York: Prentice-Hall.

Jersild, A. T. and F. B. Holmes, *Children's Fears*. Bureau of Publications, Teachers College, Columbia University, New York, 1935.

Kemp, Charles F., *The Church: The Gifted and Retarded Child*. St. Louis: Bethany Press, 1957.

Lambert, Clara, *Understand Your Child — From 6 to 12*. New York: Public Affairs Pamphlets, 22 E. 38th Street.

Le Masters, Ersel, "The Crisis of the First Baby," *Redbook*, May, 1961, p. 30.

Manwell, E. M. and S. L. Fahs, *Consider the Children — How They Grow*. Boston: The Beacon Press, 1940.

Merry, F. K. and R. V. Merry, *From Infancy to Adolescence*. New York: Harper and Brothers, 1940.

Palmer, Charles E., *The Church and the Exceptional Person.* Nashville: Abingdon Press, 1961.

Peterson, Sigurd D., *Retarded Children: God's Children.* Philadelphia: Westminster Press, 1960.

Thorpe, Louis P., *Child Psychology and Development.* New York: Ronald Press Company, 1962.

Toulle, Ellen, *Your Child's Growth, Health, and Happiness.* New York: Alfred A. Knopf.

FAMILY TOGETHER; GENERAL FAMILY LIVING

Abel, Dorothy L., *Making Housekeeping Easy.*

Adams, Charlotte, *Home Entertaining.*

Adler, Afred., *Understanding Human Nature.* Greenberg.

Agee, James, *A Death in the Family.* New York: McDowell, Obolensky, Inc., 1957

Allport, Gordon, *The Individual and His Religion.* New York: Macmillan.

Anshen, Ruth N., *The Family: Its Function and Destiny.* New York: Harper and Brothers, 1949.

Banks, Murray, *How to Live With Yourself.* New York: Prentice-Hall.

Beers, Clifford W., *A Mind That Found Itself.* Doubleday.

Benedict, Agnes and Adele Franklin, *The Happy Home.* New York: Appleton-Century.

Bowen, Elizabeth, *Friends and Relations.* Toronto: The Dial Press, 1931.

Bundesen, Herman N., *Toward Manhood.* Lippincott.

Burton, Joe W., *The Church and Family Life.* Nashville: Broadman.

Carnegie, Dale, *How to Win Friends and Influence People.* New York: Simon and Schuster, 1937.

Duvall, Evelyn M., *Family Living.* New York: New York Association Press, 1949.

Ellenwood, James E., *There Is No Place Like Home.* New York: Charles Scribner's Sons, 1938.

English, O. S. and G. H. Pearson, *Common Neuroses of Children and Adults.* Norton.

————, *Emotional Problems of Living.* Norton.

Flescher, Joachim, *Mental Health and the Prevention of Neurosis.* Liveright.

Foucher, Albert B., *Getting a Job and Getting Ahead.* New York: McGraw-Hill Book Company, 1931.

Gilbreath, Frank Bunker, Jr., and E. M. D. Carey, *Cheaper by the Dozen.* New York: Thomas Y. Crowell, 1949.

Grossman, Jean Schick, *Life With Family.* New York: Appleton-Century.

Groves, E. R., *The Family and Its Relationships.* Philadelphia: J. B. Lippincott and Company, 1932.

Havighurst, Robert J., *Ways of Growth Toward Christian Objectives.* Chicago: University of Chicago, Committee on Human Development, 1956.

Hulme, William E., *The Pastoral Care of Families.* Nashville: Abingdon Press, 1962.

Kirkendall, Lester and Arthur Gravatt, *Sex Ways — in Fact and Faith: Bases for Christian Family Policy.*

Kirkpatrick, Clifford, *The Family: As Process and Institution.* New York: Ronald Press, 1963.

Leavell, Martha Boone, *Building a Christian Home.* Nashville: Convention Press, 1952.

Levy, John and Ruth Monroe, *The Happy Family.* New York: Alfred A. Knopf, 1938.

Menninger, Karl A. and J. L. Menninger, *Love Against Hate.* Harcourt Brace.

Moore, Bernice M. and Dorothy Leahy, *You and Your Family.* Boston: D. S. Heath, 1948.

Nickell, Paulena and Jean Muir Dorsey, *Management in Family Living.*

Pratt, Dallas, *Mental Health Is a Family Affair.* New York: Public Affairs Pamphlets, 22 E. 38th Street.

Sapora, Allen V. and Elmer D. Mitchell, *The Theory of Play and Recreation.* New York: Ronald Press Company, 1961.

The American Family: A Factual Background. Report of the Inter-Agency Committee on Background Materials, National Conference on Family Life, Washington, U.S. Govt. Print. Off., 1949.

Thorman, George, *Broken Homes.* New York: Public Affairs Pamphlets, 22 E. 38th Street.

Tyler, Wilfred, *The Little World of Home.* Nashville: Broadman Press.

Van Ness, Bethann F., *My Family and I.* Nashville: Broadman Press, 1948.

Wood, Mildred W., *Living Together in the Family.* Washington D.C.: American Home Economics Association, 1946.

LOVE, COURTSHIP, ENGAGEMENT, PREPARATION FOR MARRIAGE, SINGLE ADULT

Bentley, Marguerite Logan, *Wedding Etiquette.*

Boone, William Cooke, *Together.* Nashville: Broadman Press.

Burton, Joe W., *Tomorrow You Marry.* Nashville: Broadman Press, 1950.

Crouch, W. Perry, *Guidance for Christian Home Life.* Nashville: Broadman Press, 1955.

Dahlberg, Edwin, *Youth and the Homes of Tomorrow.* Philadelphia: Judson Press.

Duvall, Evelyn M. and Reuben Hill, *When You Marry.* Boston: Heath and Company, 1945.

Duvall, Sylvanus M., *Before You Marry.* New York: New York Association Press, 1949.

Eckert, Ralph, *So You Think It's Love.* New York: Public Affairs Pamphlets, 22 E. 38th Street.

Elisa, Andrew D., "Teamwork in Premarital Counseling," *Pastoral Psychology.* December, 1959.

Jaeck, Dorothea and Gordon, *I Take Thee.* Grand Rapids: Zondervan Publishing House, 1967.

Jauncey, James H., *Magic in Marriage.* Grand Rapids, Zondervan Publishing House, 1966.

McLeod, Edith Thorton, *The Bride's Book.*

Miles, Herbert, *Sexual Happiness in Marriage.* Grand Rapids: Zondervan Publishing House, 1967.

Morris, J. Kenneth, *Premarital Counseling: A Manual for Ministers.* Englewood Cliffs: Prentice-Hall, Inc., 1960.

Phelps, Ralph A., *Blueprint for Tomorrow.* Nashville: Broadman.

Rosengarten, William, *Choosing Your Life Work.* New York: McGraw Book Company, 1924.

Strain, Frances, *Love at the Threshold.* New York: Appleton-Century Company, 1952.

Wright, Jeanne, *The Wedding Book.*

MARRIAGE

Adams, Theodore F. and Donald F. Ackland, *Marriage With Two Strikes Against It.* Nashville: Broadman Press.

———, *Making Your Marriage Succeed.* New York: Harper.

Baeck, Leo, *The Book of Marriage*. New York: Harcourt Brothers and Company, 1926.

Black, Algernon D., *If I Marry Outside My Religion*. New York: Public Affairs Committee, Inc., 1954.

Bowman, Henry A., *Marriage for Moderns*. New York: McGraw-Hill Book Company, Inc., 1954.

Burkhart, Carl, *The Secret of a Happy Marriage*. New York: Harper, 1949.

Christensen, Harold T., *Marriage Analysis — Foundations for Successful Family Life*. New York: Ronald Press Company, 1958.

Duvall, Evelyn, *Building Your Marriage*. New York: Public Affairs Pamphlets, 22 E. 38th Street.

Eisenstein, Victor, *Neurotic Interaction in Marriage*. New York: Basic Books, Inc., 1956.

Foster, Robert G., *Marriage and Family Relationships*. New York: The Macmillan Company, 1950.

Fox, Joseph L., *How to Keep Happily Married*.

Geiseman, *Making Yours a Happy Marriage*, 1946.

Goldstein, Sidney E., *Marriage and Family Counseling*. New York: McGraw-Hill Book Company, Inc., 1945.

Groves, Ernest R., *Conserving Marriage and the Family*. New York: The Macmillan Company, 1944.

Groves, E. R., *Wholesome Marriage*. Boston: Houghton-Mifflin, 1927.

Groves, Gladys H., *Marriage and Family Life*. New York: Reynal and Hitchcock, 1942.

Hamilton, G. W., *What Is Wrong With Marriage*. New York: Olber and Charles Born, 1929.

Klein, R. A. and B. J. Schuman, *How to Have a Baby — Techniques for Fertile Marriages*. Hermitage House.

Landis, Judson and Mary Landis, *Building a Successful Marriage*. New York: Prentice-Hall, Inc., 1948.

Landis, Paul H., *Making the Most of Marriage*. New York: Appleton-Century-Crofts, 1955.

————, *Your Marriage and Family Living*. New York: McGraw-Hill Book Company, 1946.

Leavell, Martha Boone, *Christian Marriage*. Nashville: Broadman Press.

Mace, David R., *Success in Marriage*. Nashville: Abingdon Press, 1958.

Magoun, F. O., *Love and Marriage.*

Mead, Margaret, *Male and Female.* Morrow and Company.

Merrill, Francis E., *Courtship and Marriage.* New York: Alfred A. Knopf, 1938.

Mudd, Emily H., *The Practice of Marriage Counseling.* New York: Association Press, 1951.

Nimkoff, Meyer, *Marriage and the Family.* New York: Houghton-Mifflin, 1947.

Owen, Jean Z., *Widows Can Be Happy.* Greenberg.

Rosen, James Alan, *Fertility in Men and Women — the How and Why of Having Children.* Coward-McCann.

Skidmore, Rex A., Hulds Van Streeter Garrett, and C. Jay Skidmore, *Marriage Consulting.* New York: Harper and Brothers, 1956.

Stokes, Walter R., *Modern Pattern for Marriage.*

Smith, *This Love of Ours.* Nashville: Cokesbury, 1947.

Stone, Hannah and Abraham, *Marriage Manual,* 1952.

Strain, Frances, *Love at the Threshold.* New York: Appleton-Century Company, 1952.

Whitman, Howard, *Let's Tell the Truth About Sex.* Pelligrini and Cudahy.

Winter, Gibson, *Love and Conflict: New Patterns in Family Life.* New York: Doubleday and Company, Inc., 1958.

Wood, *How Love Grows Into Marriage.* Nashville: Broadman.

MIDDLE ADULT

Crohn, Burrill B., *Understand Your Ulcer.* Sheridan House.

Hirsch, Edwin W., *Prostate Gland Disorder.* Greenberg.

Howe, Reuel, *Man's Need and God's Action.* Greenwich: Seabury Press, 1953.

Kordel, Lelord, *Eat and Grow Younger.* World Press.

Lasser, L. K. and Sylvia F. Porter, *How to Live Within Your Income.* New York: King Syndicate.

Liebman, Joshua L., *Peace of Mind.* Simon and Schuster.

Lippman, Caro W. and Margaret Lippman, *Understanding Your Migraine Headache.* Greenberg.

Preston, George H., *The Substance of Mental Health.* Rinehart.

Rollo, May, *The Meaning of Anxiety.* New York: Ronald Press.

Saul, Leon J., *Emotional Maturity.* New York: Lippincott.

Steincrohn, Peter J., *How to Keep Fit Without Exercise.* Wilfred Fund.

Stewart, Maxwell S., *Women — and Their Money*. New York: Public Affairs Pamphlets, 22 E. 38th Street.

Wool, Harold, *Trends in Pattern of Working Life, 1900 to 1975*. Monthly Labor Review, Vol. 71, Oct., 1950, pp. 438-442.

Yeaxley, Basil A., *Religion and the Growing Mind*. Digswell Place: James Nisbit and Company, 1959.

OLDER ADULT; RETIREMENT

Albrecht, Ruth, "The Social Roles of Old People." *Journal of Gerontology*, Vol. 6, April, 1951, pp. 138-145.

Close, Kathryn, "Grandpa Wants to Work." *Survey Graphic*, Vol. 37, June, 1948, pp. 288-292.

Donahue, Wilma and Clark Tibbitts, *Planning the Older Years*. Ann Arbor: University of Michigan Press, 1950.

English, Spurgeon O., "A Brighter Future for Old People." *Geriatrics*, Vol. 4, July-August, 1949, pp. 217-224.

Gray, Madeline, *The Changing Years*. New York: Doubleday.

Hunter, Woodrow W., "A Proposed Activity Center for Older People." *Geriatrics*, Vol. 6, March-April, 1951, pp. 121-128.

Lawton, George, *Aging Successfully*. New York: Columbia University Press.

Lawton, George and Maxwell S. Stewart, *When You Grow Older*. New York: Public Affairs Pamphlets, 22 E. 38th Street.

Marris, Peter, *Widows and Their Families*. London: Routledge and Kegan Paul, 1958.

Maves, Paul B., *Older People and the Church*. Nashville: Abingdon-Cokesbury Press, 1949.

Monroe, Robert T., *Diseases in Old Age*. New Haven: Harvard University Press.

Neisser, Edith, *How to Be a Good Mother-in-Law and Grandmother*. New York: Public Affairs Pamphlets, 22 E. 38th Street.

Never Too Old. New York (State) Legislature, Newburgh: Joint Committee on Problems of the Aging, 1949 (Legislative Document No. 32, 1949).

Pan, Ju-Shu, "Personal Adjustment of Old People in Church Homes for the Aged." *Geriatrics*, Vol. 5, May-June, 1950, pp. 166-170.

Potter, Robert D., *Arthritis*. Dodd, Mead and Company.

"The Problem of the Older Worker." Canada: Department of Labor, *Labour Gazette*, Vol. 47, September, 1947, pp. 1251-1258.

Salomon, I., *Retire and Be Happy.* Greenberg.

Shock, Nathan W., "Older People and Their Potentialities for Gainful Employment." *Journal of Gerontology,* Vol. 2, April, 1947, pp. 93-102.

Slichter, Sumner H., "Rewards for Deferred Retirement." *Economic Security* (Chamber of Commerce of the USA), Vol. 7, April-May, 1950, pp. 35-38.

Smith, Philip M., "Employment Handicaps of Older Workers." *American Journal of Economics and Sociology,* Vol. 8, January, 1949, pp. 117-123.

Trends in Retirement Planning. New York: American Management Association, 1948 (Insurance Series No. 73).

PARENTS

Alexander, Franz, *Fundamentals of Psychoanalysis.* Norton.

Carson, Ruth, *So You Want to Adopt a Baby.* New York: Public Affairs Pamphlets, 22 E. 38th Street.

Davenport, M., *Heredity in Relation to Eugenics.* Henry Holt and Company, 1911.

Egleson, Jim and Janet, *Parents Without Partners.* New York: Dutton and Company, Inc., 1961.

Ellenwood, James E., *Just and Durable Parents.* New York: Charles Scribner's Sons, 1948.

French, Edward L. and J. Clifford Scott, *Child in the Shadows: A Manual for Parents of Retarded Children.* New York: J. B. Lippincott, 1960.

Gruenberg, Sidonie M., *We, the Parents.* New York: Harper.

Overton, Grace Sloan, *Living With Parents.* Nashville: Broadman.

Popenoe, Paul, *Applied Eugenics.* New York: Macmillan Company, 1933.

Stern, Edith M. and Elsa Castendyck, *The Handicapped Child: A Guide for Parents.* A. A. Wyn.

Symonds, P. M., *The Psychology of Parent-Child Relationships.* New York: Appleton-Century-Crofts, Inc., 1939.

Wiggom, Elbert Edward, *The Fruit of the Family Tree.* New York: The Bobbs Merrill Company.

Wolf, Ann W. M., *Parents' Manual.* Simon and Schuster.

Yahraes, Herbert, *Planning Your Family.* New York: Public Affairs Pamphlets, 22 E. 38th Street.

INDEX

Ackland, Donald F. 89
adolescent, adolescence 16, 18, 28, 64-83, 118
adulthood 115-124, 134
adults:
  single 26-30
  middle adults 28, 66, 113, 115
  older adults 133-146
  senility, senescence 67, 117, 118, 119, 120, 126
affection 86, 93
age of accountability 58
Allport, Gordon 73
American Association for Adult Education 122
avocational 140

baby-sit, sitters 127
behavior 90, 123, 130
Bible 34, 35, 37, 58, 70, 78, 91, 92, 96, 101, 102, 111
boy 53-54
Browning, Robert 114
business 116, 118, 125

child, children 43, 46-47, 51, 87, 88, 95-97, 104, 116, 118, 122, 125, 127, 131
children's worker 43, 56
Christian home emphases 92, appendix
church 20, 27, 28, 30, 35, 70, 85, 93, 95, 98, 115, 116, 131, 135, 140
college 118, 125
communication 84, 125, 132
community 27, 46, 113
conformity 69-70
conversation 15, 16, 17, 32, 36-38, 40, 74-76, 86, 102, 113, 114, 119, 129, 132
conversion 56-59, 107

counseling 21-22, 29
counselor 40
courtship 14, 17, 22, 39, 40, 41
creative thinking 76

dating 14-17, 41
Deen, Edith 91
denominational 115
dialogue 13-18, 84, 113, 119, 125, 133
discipline 50-55, 72, 80, 88, 118
discussion 32
dissatisfaction 81
divorce 130, 147 ff
Drakeford, John 20

education 85, 116, 122
emotions, emotional 18, 38, 74-76, 114, 130, 133
engagement 17, 18, 20, 21, 23, 32, 39, 133
environment 95
evangelism 44, 47
example 96

family 17, 18, 19, 25, 26, 29, 34, 39, 45, 47, 61, 84-112, 117, 126
father 44, 87-90
father-mother role 44-47, 86
fear 66, 134
fellowship 84, 98, 99, 102, 132
finances, financial 18, 39, 40, 71, 135, 138, 145
friendship 14, 128, 141, 142
Freud 90

government 115, 121
grandchildren 118, 125, 126, 131
grandparent 118, 126, 127, 128
guidance 19-22, 29, 44, 50, 73-74, 126
guilt 37, 58, 115, 123

179

handicaps 120, 134
Herget, John F. 64
Hogg Foundation 121
home 20, 25, 26, 33, 34, 37, 41, 46, 50, 75, 85, 94, 97, 102, 103, 111
honeymoon 31-33, 133
Howe, Reuel 36, 86
human development 66-73
Hurlock, Elizabeth 87

imitation 76
independence 56-57, 83, 94
industry, industrialists 116, 123
infant 49, 87, 94

jobs 44, 91, 131, 139

learning 94-97, 100, 106, 122
literature 76-80
loneliness 135
love 13, 14, 17, 22-24, 92, 104, 110, 133

marriage:
   adjustments within 31, 33-35, 38, 39, 44, 94, 113
   preparation for 20, 21, 24-26
   sacredness 41-42
   selection 13-18, 73, 76
materialism 80, 115
maturity 18, 19, 36, 38, 40, 48, 59, 72, 115, 116, 120, 130
Maves, Paul B. 120
melloescence 118
military service 41
moonlighting 131
mother 44-47, 49, 90-94, 114, 125, 133
Mozes, M. D. 36
Munro, Harry C. 57

National Family Week 20

Oates, Wayne 21
Oliver, Bernard J. 114
Overton, Grace 71

parents 19, 28, 43-63, 64-83, 86, 87-94, 101-102, 104, 111, 118, 126, 127
partners 88, 92, 128, 130, 131

pastor 21, 29, 116
patriarchial 118, 126
Payne, Vera Minga 137
personality 15, 18, 19, 25, 32, 52, 60, 66, 72, 96, 130
prayer 101, 102-105
preoccupation 118, 124, 125-126, 128, 129
professional 116

recreation 85, 98-99, 100, 142, 143
religion 37
retirement 113, 114, 129, 133-146
rewards 62

sacrifice 48, 105
school 20, 73, 95, 96
secure, security 61, 82, 90, 99, 103, 116, 134, 135, 140
self 49, 59, 118, 129
self-confidence 59-61, 71
self-control 119
self-evaluation 118
self-understanding 118, 119
sharing 84, 92
sin 80-83
social 82, 86, 100, 114
spiritual love 23
status 86
Stolz, Karl R. 134
success 115
Sutherland, Robert L. 121
symbolism 68-70, 72

teen-agers 64-83, 95, 108, 120, 128, 131
testing 21, 108
Thorndike, E. L. 122
Trueblood, Elton 84
Truett, George W. 79

vacation 100
values 84
virescence 118
vocation 74, 115, 116, 128, 135

worship (family) 84, 85, 88, 89, 90, 101, 102-112

young married couples 35, 36, 38
youth worker 21